This book is a culmination of years of practice and observation. It was, without a doubt, the most difficult mental endeavor of my life. As much hard work as I put into this book, it would not have been possible without a number of incredible people.

First, my amazing wife Ana, who took turns sleeping in shifts with me to proofread so we could make the release date.

Second, thank you to all of those who subscribed and shared my videos. Without you, none of this would have been possible and I would have likely never had the time to complete this book.

Next, thank you to my wonderful cousin April, who convinced me to pursue my dreams when I was ready to give up and take the "sensible" path. Sometimes all it takes is someone with the right words at the right time.

And last, to my long- time heroes Bruce Lee and Muhammad Ali, who taught myself and many others like me that martial arts is, above all, a means of self-expression.

How To Use This Book

This book aims to provide the first comprehensive list of footwork in combat sports and martial arts as a whole, and (equally importantly) to explain the reasoning and intentions behind these footwork techniques and patterns. As such, the primary purpose from the start of the book is to identify superior positions from which you can gain an advantage over your opponent, and then identify specific patterns you can use to achieve these positions. Each pattern, position and technique are explained at length through thorough written description and pictures. Arrows, circles and other markers have been inserted into the photos for more clarity. Furthermore, for nearly every technique an example is given of a noteworthy fighter using said technique during one of their fights. If beneficial, the exact round and time the fighter used the footwork sequence is noted. A majority of these fights can be found online for free, and any that are not can be viewed on the website of the organization that owns the rights to show it. These real-life examples can help the reader to fine tune the distance and timing; especially because I have slightly exaggerated many of the movements in the pictures to help keep each step distinct. In this way, the reader first learns what the footwork pattern is and what it may be used for. Then they are able to study a clear step-by-step demonstration through the pictures so that they can practice it efficiently, and then can look up an example of the technique being used by a professional fighter.

Table of Contents

Chapter 1 – Fundamentals of Movement_____Pg. 2

Chapter 2 – Footwork Techniques_____Pg. 9

Chapter 3 – Strategy_____Pg 85

Chapter 4 – Superior Positions_____Pg. 127

Chapter 5 – Basic & Advanced Footwork Sequences_____Pg. 163

Footwork Wins Fights - Footwork For Boxing, Kickboxing, Martial Arts & MMA

Chapter 1 - Fundamentals of Movement

Before exploring the world of patterns, angles and strategies, it's important to have a basic understanding about a few fundamentals of movement in regards to footwork. In other words, it's vital to understand which techniques your will body to move as efficiently as possible. Most footwork techniques rely on speed and smooth transitions from step to step. Add onto this the fact that superior footwork movements lead to superior striking, both in regards to power and fluidity, and it becomes apparent that quality of movement should be high on any fighters list of training priorities.

You may notice that a few of these rules are similar or in fact the same as the ones in my book on power generation. Once again, solid footwork fundamentals will help you build speed, power and structure. This holds true throughout any punch, kick, takedown, or clinch you may attempt. In other words: without footwork, there is nothing.

The Basics of A Stance

The stance is everything. It's the means through which your power, strength, movement and balance all work together. Some stances are best for defense, some for offense, some for mobility, others for structure. Some stances are best for striking while some are best for wrestling. Some stances are best for moving forward, others for retreating, and others still for lateral movement.

Whichever footwork you choose to use, it must match up with your stance. There are several variables to keep in mind.

A lower center of balance allows for more stability.

Fighters who crouch low will hold firmer and stay more solid to the ground. Steps will lack speed, but will be grounded and balanced.

A higher center of balance allows for greater mobility.

Think of fighters like Muhammad Ali or Dominick Cruz. The higher weight distribution allows for greater freedom of movement. It is very easy for such fighters to lose their balance, especially if they get caught mid step. Wrestlers as well as swarming, bullrushing brawlers are always a major concern for such fighters.

A narrow, sideways stance allows for better Linear (In and out) movement.

A "bladed" stance allows fighters to get in and out very quickly. Think of fighters like Conor McGregor, Sugar Ray Leonard or Machida. Great for setting up a one-two, sidekick, or nearly any linear strike. It does delay the rear hand and foot by keeping it further away from the target, giving it longer to travel. This often facilitates a larger step and greater preparatory movement to land with the rear hand or foot. It does, however, ease the burden of preparing spinning movements off of the rear leg (like spin back kicks or spin back fists). A smaller step inside will be needed, if it is needed at all. This stance may make it much more difficult to cut off the cage.

A squared up, forward stance allows for better Lateral (sideways) movement.

Like a low stance, this stance is often more stable. It makes it easier to sprawl, but harder to turn. It puts both hands close to their targets, so it's a great stance for aggressive fighters. It's also ideal for grounded punches off of lateral movement. A forward stance is also great for wrestlers. It limits the range they need to shoot, and helps them cover distance as quickly as possible.

The closer your feet are to each other, the easier it will be to change direction.

Closer Feet Means More Freedom of Movement

This has a lot to do with a higher center of gravity, but putting your feet closer together also allows you to adjust your weight and move in different directions with greater speed. With your feet closer together, it is easier to bounce, or burst into a low stance.

The Wider Apart Your Feet, the More Stability.

More stability helps you hold your ground and structure your strikes. You may not be able to move as easily, but you will essentially be more "solid".

The direction in which you distribute your weight is the direction in which it will be easiest to move.

Keeping Your Weight Forward Eases Forward Motion

A pressure fighter will not want to keep the weight on their back foot, it will make it too difficult to move forward. A fighter who constantly circles left will not want to keep their weight right most of the time. Leaning over too far to the right will inhibit their ability to move left. Over time you will want to pay close attention to where you distribute your weight in exchanges. Add on feints and head movements to ease the transition into your movements, especially your beginning attacks.

Stepping - Heel vs Toes

Runners have been arguing about this forever as well. It's a large part of technique which nearly every martial art has a strong opinion on. So much so that both Jack Dempsey and Miyamoto Musashi took the time to talk at length about it in their books. Stepping on your heel gives you a more solid base, and lets you come down "heavier". Fighters who step on their heel include Archie Moore, Jack Dempsey, Bruce Lee, Bas Rutten, and Miyamoto Musashi. It's great for styles that prefer more weight on the lead foot.

Staying more on your toes is "lighter", allowing for more mobility. You will be able to change directions easier, and pivot or turn into kicks and punches faster. Fighters who use this technique are Vasyl Lomachenko, TJ Dillashaw, Wonderboy Thompson, Muhammad Ali, and many others.

It is best to really think about this simple, but important, aspect as the first step in defining your style. A "heavier", grounded fighter may prefer to stay on his heels. An in and out fighter who likes to circle and rapidly change angles will undoubtedly prefer to stay up on his toes more. Many styles prefer the rear heel be raise higher, to help push off when attacking. Others prefer the weight on the back leg, with the front heel raised higher to ease lead leg kicks and checks.

That being said, there is nothing that says you can't step both ways, or change up your steps for certain attacks. But keep in mind that an integrated system where an attack can be thrown off of any step or without adjusting your stance is always best. This will lower your reaction time, speed up your movements, and make your style seem "smooth" and "seamless."

Sliding vs Lifting

Some fighters prefer to lift their feet off of the ground with each step, some prefer to slide their feet along the ground to it's correct position. Sliding your foot keeps you "smoother" and more grounded. Lifting your foot allows for faster movement.

Bouncing & Hopping

It will be assumed throughout the book that most steps will be performed in the usual manner, one foot following the other. But it is possible to bounce off of both feet at the same time for many of the footwork patterns outlined. Karate practitioners and TKD practitioners do this all the time. There are some benefits. Bouncing facilitates faster kicking, as it completely frees your hips to turn or spin. It also lets you adjust your feet faster, and allows you to work rhythm manipulations and feints right into your base movements. Considerations include the fact that it is not as solid, does not allow for a medium (let alone a low) base, and drains a lot of energy very quickly.

Where do you stand?

When it comes to stances, once again it is best to choose one that goes towards furthering your purpose. You have probably already been taught a stance that blends well into the movements of whichever discipline that you follow. But it is always good to stop and think about your personal preferences and strengths while fighting, and make adjustments to aid you further. Even if the adjustments are small, like putting a little more weight onto your lead foot or not crouching quite as low, they can make a big difference. Everyone is different, experiment for yourself.

It should be said that it is possible to combine many of these elements together. Fighters who can move around on their toes and then sink down into their punch are very few, but they are particularly dangerous. Especially so if they are able to quickly dart forward from a high, narrow stance and then sink down deep into an attack. Sugar Ray Robinson was a prime example of this ability. He could circle smoothly on his toes, methodically picking his opponent apart, before leaping in and sinking down to deliver some of the most terrifying punches ever captured on film. Experimenting for yourself will help you to figure out what works best for you.

Chapter 2 - Footwork Techniques

Stepping

Stepping is the most basic and most common way to move in a fight. It helps preserve energy making it very economic. It can also be used to make small, subtle adjustments, or to Enter into an Exchange aggressively.

Basic Stepping

As a general rule, the foot closest to the direction you wish to travel in will move first when stepping. The other foot will then adjust to establish your preferred stance. In other words, when moving forward, your front foot will move first. When moving backwards, your rear foot. When moving left, your left foot will step out first before your right foot moves to it's regular position, and when moving right, your right foot will move first as well.

Stepping Forward - Lead Foot Moves First

Stepping Back - Rear Foot Moves First

Stepping Right - Right Foot Moves First

Stepping Left - Left Foot Moves First

You will rarely if ever move entirely in a one direction. Most steps should be diagonal, as your objective is not only to attack or retreat, nor is it only to open up or close off. Many steps will involve a small pivot as well in order to stay well aligned with your competitor.

Exception - Back To Front

Some fighters, such as Joe Frazier and many Muay Thai practitioners, step their rear foot first when moving forward. This better loads the lead hand and foot by allowing a stronger push off of the back foot, like a shuffle. But it should not be mistaken for a shuffle; the steps are heavy, shorter, and have their own beat. They are not smooth. This movement pattern also facilities smoother kicks off of the lead leg by freeing the lead leg to attack with each step forward by the back leg. Using this pattern disguises this oft-necessary preparatory step by making it a common occurrence, and therefore harder to read.

<u>Stepping Forward With Rear Leg First Lets You Load Up On Your Hook</u>

With A Cross Hook Combination

Stepping your rear foot forward lets you load up your hook off your cross, helping to rapidly cover distance and, once again, load your lead hand.

Load Step

A good compromise between lead foot first and rear foot first stepping is to sneak your back foot further than normal when bringing it back into position. In other words, move forward by first lifting your front foot, in the normal method. Then, when putting your rear foot back into position, slide or step it slightly closer than normal, shortening your stance for a better push off when attacking. Lomachenko uses this technique frequently, further hiding the preparation behind a jab or jab-feint.

Stepping Forward - Slide the Rear Foot Closer to Load Up A Strike

Push Step

Rather than merely lifting your front foot, a push step is when you push hard off of your rear foot to throw a strike. This creates a more explosive transition into your strike, and it is overall just a faster way of moving.

Push Step With No Strike

Push Step Backwards With Jab

Drop Step & Trigger Step

The drop step was so important to heavyweight champion Jack Dempsey that he devoted an entire chapter of his book to it. It is simple, but hard to train the body to do with any competency. The idea is to load most of your weight onto your lead leg, guaranteeing a fast start and a lot of weight preloaded into your strike. Dempsey used this in conjunction with a Push Step or "Trigger Step" as he put it. Named so because lifting your lead foot would "trigger" the rear foot to push off hard and save you from falling. Previous to Dempsey fighters used to call these kinds of punches "jolts."

Practice "Falling" First, Lean Forward Then Lift Your Lead Foot

Now With the "Trigger Step" - Lean Forward, Then Quickly Lift Your Foot Before Exploding

This Technique Is Equally Effective With A Cross. Note That The Weight Moves Forward Before The Step

Tilt Step

Floyd Mayweather, one of the best defensive fighters ever to compete, uses this step consistently. The exact opposite of the Drop Step, the idea is to lean back and keep your weight behind you as you step forward. This does two things: First, it leaves you uncommitted to the step, making it easier to rapidly retreat, even mid step. Remember that the more weight you load in one direction, the easier it will be to move in that direction.

Weight Backwards Means An Easy Escape Even When Moving Forwards

The second benefit is that loading more weight onto your back foot sets you up for a harder blow if you do choose to attack. It does so by creating a greater transfer of weight from the back to the front foot. If you read my book Power of the Pros, you'll already know that more weight over a longer distance puts more momentum into your attacks. So even though Mayweather chooses his strikes wisely, they still pack decent power.

Half Step & Foot Feint

After stepping forward with your lead foot, quickly step or slide it back into position, regaining your initial position. There are several reasons to do this. One is to quickly move in and out of range with a lighter attack, usually a jab.

You can also use this movement as a "Foot Feint" in order to draw your opponent by countering an attack that isn't coming. By the time they've countered, you are already out of range, having stepped back immediately. If you are fortunate, they have overreached while trying to follow you back with their strike, and you can effectively counter their counter.

<u>Bring Your Foot Forward As If You Are Stepping In to Attack, Then Pull It Back to Your Primary Stance</u>

This movement is also used in conjunction with pendulum steps, as part of your preparatory pattern. More on preparatory patterns in a later chapter. You can also lunge backwards, for much the same reason. It baits your opponent into thinking you're retreating, and then you quickly step back into position to drive a hard strike into them.

Step Back With Your Rear Foot, and Then Step the Same Foot Forward Again to Your Original Position

With Pull Counter or Shoulder Roll Counter

This is a great way to get your opponent to overreach, and then catch them on the way back

Rebound Step (A Push Step Off of A Jump or Incomplete Movement)

Rebound steps are used by extreme mobility fighters like Willie Pep or TJ Dillashaw. The best way to picture a rebound step is to think of jumping from stone to stone in a pond. The idea is to push off of the ground to change direction before both feet have returned to your primary stance. Say you are stepping forward. Your lead foot touches the ground, and, rather than bringing your rear foot into position to establish your stance, you push hard off of your lead foot just as it lands to change directions.

Stepping Forward To Rebound Right, Then Left

Rather than take a second step to return to your primary stance, rebound off of your lead foot before your rear foot touches the ground. Then rebound once more off of your right.

With A Partner In The Picture, The Reason For The Angle Change Is More Apparent

Stutter Step

Stutter Steps are quickly accelerating and over emphasizing your steps in order to confuse your opponent. They are meant to feint or draw a reaction. Usually, you will be taking perhaps twice the amount of steps you normally would to cover the same amount of distance. No image for this one as it is self-explanatory and impossible to show in pictures. anyways.

You may also lift your feet higher than normal, to feint or to make an upcoming kick non-telegraphic. Stutter steps are also great for breaking rhythm, either to startle the opponent and keep them on their toes, or to create a favorable reaction before coming in with the real attack.

Linear Cross Step

This will be familiar to anyone with a background in most traditional Eastern martial arts. One foot steps past the other, but the body remains sideways, resulting in crossed legs. This can be used effectively for lead leg kicks, but is highly telegraphic. In other words, your opponent will expect what is coming. It also lacks the speed of a switch kick, where you jump into a more open or cross legged position to land the kick. That being said, this setup can put a lot of power into your kicks. Some martial arts deliver back fists or such off of this movement, but this is rarely effective in real life.

Cross Step In Front of Lead Leg to Load Up A Roundhouse Kick

Cross Step Behind Front Leg to Load Up A Side Kick

Lateral Cross Step

This is a movement pattern that is opposite of the Basic Sidestep. Rather than move the foot closest to the direction you are travelling first (if moving right, your right foot would move, if moving left, your left foot) you will instead step your left foot right, or vice versa. Crossing your legs like this can disturb your balance, limit some movements, and leave you susceptible to takedowns.

Rear Foot Steps Left Behind Leg

Lead Leg Steps Left, In Front of Right

Though it does have disadvantages a number of great fighters have used it successfully and correctly, and it does have its merits. Muhammad Ali would usually throw his jab off of this movement, whether he was dancing or not. The reason being, it allows a fighter to remain far safer while jabbing by allowing them to stay more sideways while exposing less of their body to hits.

GGG uses this footwork technique in the exact opposite way. GGG will stalk his opponent and cut off the ring by stepping his lead foot across his back. Most fighters attempt to cut off the ring by stepping their rear leg far out, squaring themselves up and blocking the opponent's escape route. However, Golovkin's style relies heavily on his well developed jab. So he maintains his sideway position and keeps his legs loaded for fast, linear motion by cross stepping towards his opponents.

As a useful tip: you can pivot off of your lead foot to follow your opponent's movements off of a cross step. However, don't confuse the two movements. A cross step moves you laterally as well as allowing you to pivot. You will know it's a true cross step and not a pivot because your lead foot will need to step at the end of the movement to regain your stance. With pivots, you will maintain the structure of your stance throughout. You can also reverse directions off of a half-completed cross step, to keep your opponent guessing.

Reverse Directions and Push Off to Change Directions Quickly

Linear Switch Step

A linear switch step puts you into the same position as a linear cross step, loading up your lead leg to kick. This technique is utilized heavily in Muay Thai. Rather than step, you will jump or slide your feet into position. Many fighters throw this with the feel of a Stutter Step. They do so by emphasising the raising of each knee up high, and stomping the ground, one foot landing slightly towards the others. Fire off your kick quickly, and do not stay with your feet crossed too long. It heavily compromises your balance. This technique is highly telegraphic, so you probably want to distract your opponent as you load up the movement (letting a jab go is a great way to raise your opponents guard and block his vision).

Pivoting

Pivoting looks easy, but is one of the hardest things to do correctly. Most people tend to lose their foundational structure and balance without even noticing they've done so. There are two ways to pivot. The fastest and but most unstable way is to raise your heel slightly and spin on your toes, while pushing off with the opposite leg.

Pivoting Inside

Another option some prefer is to turn your lead foot in or out, at the angle you wish to turn, and then swivel your body in line with it. This is a more stable method, as you are able to immediately sink your weight down on your heel after you step. This method is also more telegraphic and not as fast/smooth.

Pivoting Outside

Either movement can be combined with a step for greater mobility. For instance, you can step deep inside, ducking under your opponents counter cross, and then pivot off of your step to land a lead hook.

Pivoting is best used to follow your opponent as they circle around you, or to move into a superior angle, either offensively or defensively. Floyd Mayweather is a master of pivoting. He combines it with upper body movement to evade punches while staying close enough to be toe-to-toe with his opponents. Being able to pivot a full 90 degrees or greater is a rare skill, but highly valuable.

Pivoting Shuffle/Angled Shuffle (Lomachenko)

This is what it sounds like, a mix between a pivot and a shuffle. It's the "Matrix" like move many think of when they think of Lomachenko. To execute this difficult footwork technique first step you lead foot out, and then bring your back foot close to your front foot as you pivot off of your lead foot. Once your rear foot completes its step, you should already have turned off of your lead foot. Now push off of your back foot, continuing the same arc you began off of your pivot.

Each Step Separated For Clarity

Example: Lomachenko vs Koasicha Round 4 (Overhead View In Post Round Highlights)

All At Once

Jump Turn

This was a favorite of Mike Tyson. It is similar to a Angling Shuffle, but your feet do not come as close, and momentum is built off of more of a jump than a shuffle. Jump off of both feet and turn your body hard, realigning yourself and opening attacks off angle. By staying low and sinking your weight you can remain stable and maintain power while performing this technique. It's rare to see this performed successfully on a consistent basis from anyone other than Tyson.

Example: Tyson vs Tillis Knockdown In The 4th. (Although he much more commonly used it for more minute adjustments at close range.)

Shuffling

Forward/Backwards

Shuffling gets you to your destination faster than a step, and allows you to cover more distance. When stepping, most fighters move their front foot first to move forward, and back foot first to move backwards. When shuffling, the exact opposite is true. The back foot slides up to the front before the front foot move back into place to it's normal position, and vice versa. However, adding a slight forward step to the beginning of your forward shuffle or a slight backwards step to the beginning of your backwards shuffle can speed up the movement.

Shuffling Backwards

Lateral Shuffle

This is a sideways shuffle from a Neutral position. It is primarily used to quickly circle the ring. You will see Ali and Sugar Ray Leonard circle outside in this manner. You can remain unpredictable and bait your opponent by quickly changing directions.

   This is a good way to escape the ropes or cage, especially since the close proximity to the edge will likely put you into a more squared up, neutral stance anyways. Lateral shuffles are often continuations of L-Steps, and allow you to easily spring forward from any angle with either foot in front. Demetrious Johnson is a big fan of this technique. At close range, a lateral shuffle can help exit an Exchange in which you have squared your body up to grapple or strike. Think of Ali shuffling out after landing a cross. It can also be used to readjust off-angle before continuing an exchange. All of these techniques will be covered in later chapters.

Half Shuffle/Pendulum Step

The term Pendulum step has come to mean two different things in different martial arts. We will differentiate them by referring to this technique as a Pendulum Step, and the technique used to quickly deliver kicks as a Pendulum Shuffle, explained below.

The Pendulum Step is the act of drawing your lead foot back towards your rear foot, and then putting it back into place to reestablish your stance. This is probably the most common preparatory footwork pattern seen in combat sports. We will get into preparatory patterns in a later chapter, but the purpose of them is to get your opponents used to certain movement patterns so as to disguise your real entries, as well as keeping you mobile (among other uses.) The Pendulum Step is remarkably useful because it blends into a number of Entries, making is a seamless transition into a great deal of attacks. It also transitions well into retreating footwork techniques such as L-Steps. Used in conjunction with Foot Feints, the Pendulum Step has been invaluable for In-Out fighters for a very, very long time.

Example: Ray Leonard vs Luis Vega (Leonard used this technique to play with distance and rhythm.)

The Pendulum Step is not purely a linear movement. Much like Basic Steps, they are not limited to linear or lateral movements, but can be done at any angle.

Another consideration: You can place your lead foot all the way back to your rear foot to disguise shuffles and L-Steps, or move it back only a few inches. It depends what you are trying to set up. It's also a great way to pull your leg back out of the way of a leg kick without breaking your movement. After all, a major disadvantage of checking a kick is that it leaves you mostly immobile.

Pendulum Shuffle

Not to be confused with a Pendulum Step, which is explained in detail above. A Pendulum Shuffle usually begins with your weight forward. The lead foot lifts first, and the rear foot pushes forward. However, rather than let your weight fall forward, you will instead lean back, raising your knee high.

Example: Wonderboy Thompson vs Rory MacDonald (Thompson used this technique to set up his non-telegraphic kicks from long range.)

That is because the purpose of a Pendulum Shuffle is primarily to set up a non-telegraphic kick. It eliminates the need to take any preparatory steps first. The best uses for Pendulum Shuffles are to set up linear strikes, like sidekicks to the leg or body. These are great "distance keepers", keeping an opponent at arm's length. They are also great for intercepting attacks that require more preparation from the opponent, especially when an opponent opens his centerline by squaring up. They can lack hip rotation, making it difficult to add much power to curving kicks. However, setting up a low roundhouse to the shin or ankle can be advantageous, as it possesses enough power to disrupt the opponents balance as they step in. Look at any Wonderboy Thompson or Bill Superfoot Wallace fight to see the aforementioned techniques used effectiv. Pendulum Shuffles blend well with Pendulum Steps, Basic Steps, and Stutter Steps.

L- Step

Named so because it makes the shape of an L. The first half is basically an ordinary linear shuffle, but the second half is a lateral shuffle. Over time, you can train these two movements to blend into each other, both feet leaving the air simultaneously .Once you have this down, it's a great way to move offline and to retreat instantaneously. It blends in well with Pendulum Steps, and is especially useful for avoiding leg kicks while opening up a new angle of attack.

Example: Leonard vs Hagler (Leonard used this technique to change angles every time Hagler got settled.)

Upon completing the L - Step, you can step your lead foot back into position to assume your regular stance, or continue to laterally shuffle around the ring.

L - Shift

With L - Steps, the lead foot steps back, and then the rear foot steps out. If your right foot is back (Orthodox Stance) you will step right. If your left foot is back (Southpaw Stance) you will step left. With L - Shifts, the lead foot still steps in, but then the lead foot steps again. The same rule applies. If your lead foot is your left foot, you will step left, and vice versa. This step is not near as smooth but is advantageous for fighters comfortable with either foot forward. Demetrious Johnson uses this "Reverse L – Step" a great deal.

Example: Demetrious Johnson vs Wilson Reis (Johnson used both L-Steps and L-Shifts to change stances and the direction he was circling effectively throughout the fight.)

Once you have stepped out with your lead foot, you can stay in a more Neutral stance and laterally shuffle around the ring, pivot back into your beginning stance, or change stances from orthodox to southpaw or vice versa.

C - Shift

Used premerally in Karate (usually called C-Steps), the C - Shift was also highly utilized by Willie Pep, and is still used today by Dominick Cruz and Demetrious Johnson. The first half of a C - Shift is performed the exact same as a regular shuffle. But after the rear foot moves to the front, it continues, shifting forward and making the shape of a C. This pattern is almost non-existent in combat sports, so we will only pay attention to the backwards variation, which is great for circling the ring (check out Willie Pep) and can be used to drive opponents into punches.

C Shift Backwards

Example: Willie Pep vs Ray Famechon (Pep used this technique to circle the ring, evade Famechon, and drive him into his rear hand when he gave chase.)

Add On A Rebound Step To Catch Your Opponent Coming In

This is technically one of the least efficient ways to change stances. Not only does it take a longer path than a regular shift, it compromises your structure and balance by unnecessarily placing your feet together. However, for movement based fighters, who rely on being unpredictable, it is a great fit. It blends well with L - Steps, Reverse L - Steps, Shuffles, Pendulum Steps, and V - Shifts (see below), leaving the fighter unpredictable and his moves non-telegraphic. It is not as dangerous when being used to circle at long range, but it's not a great idea at close or mid range.

V - Shift

Like the last three footwork variations, V - Shifts are performed off of a half shuffle. However, after the lead foot steps back, the rear foot moves forward to change stances. You will have stayed in basically the same spot, the only difference is that you will have changed stances. Additionally, you can step your lead foot forward, and then step your other foot backwards.

V Shift Forwards

Example: Dom Cruz vs Scott Jorgenson (Cruz used this technique to exit off of his wide hooks, leaving Jorgensen off balance and confused.)

Add On Rebound And Punch

V Shift Backwards

Example: Dom Cruz vs Urijah Faber 3 Cruz took Faber down with a V-Shift in Round 1.)

From Southpaw

This is a great way to surprise someone who has been stalking or chasing you. To set up this entry, get your opponent used to chasing you, then V - Shift into a superior position (V - Step sequences are covered in a later chapter) and throw hard to take them by surprise.

Shifting

Shifting is when you change stances, from Orthodox to Southpaw or Vice Versa. This can help you change angles, to take Superior Positions, cut off the cage, Draw opponents into attacks, or rapidly cover distance.

Step Through

The simplest form of shifting. Simply step your rear leg forward, changing from orthodox to southpaw or vice versa. Shifting leaves many temporary openings as you transition between stances, but is also allows you to set up new lines of attack while offering more defensive mobility.

Doubling Up And Moving To The Outside Works Well

Example: Roberto Duran vs Anyone. The version shown is much more common in MMA, along with an Overhand to Double Leg, but Duran used it in conjunction with a left hook to the body to get inside.)

Effective defensive techniques must be added to this step to minimize the potential danger and take full advantage of this movement. Head movement, a competent guard, and excellent timing will all help. All of these should supplement your offensive techniques. Shifting should primarily be done while striking or initiating a takedown. One of it's premiere uses is catching an elusive opponent. Another is to take an opponent by surprise, attacking them from an angle they do not expect.

The Double Shift - Dempsey Roll

This technique should be used against an opponent who has been constantly retreating straight back. Put your full wight into every strike by shifting side to side. The first shift should knock down your opponents guard, and the second should catch them flush.

The Dempsey Roll

Example: Jack Dempsey vs Jess Willard (Be warned, this fight is the worst recorded beating to ever happen in a ring. It's not pretty.)

Be sure your opponent does not know the Anti Dempsey Roll before throwing this...

You can see Tyson do the Dempsey roll twice at the very beginning of his fight against Eddie Richardson.

Karate Style Blitz

Karate like Blitzes are better for adding on kicks but can lack defense.

Jump Shift

Commonly used in TKD tournaments, the jump shift is one of the quickest ways to switch stances, and allows you to stay in place while doing so. As such, this technique is ideal for setting up rear leg kicks, usually by switching into an open stance from a closed stance. It can also be used defensively, turning from an open position where you are more vulnerable to rear side attacks, to a closed stance, which puts your shoulder, hip and arm in the way of power shots. When watching an Olympic TKD match you can see both fighters switch from stance to stance multiple times, trying to set up an angle and avoid getting caught.

But aside from this specific and more complex use, this technique can also be used as a fast, low effort way to change stancing while moving around the mat. Especially true if you happen to prefer switching stances for tactical reasons.

Switch Shift

While a Jump Switch has more of a "turning" feel, with your feet leaving the ground to let your hips swing through, the Switch Shift feels more like a Step Through shift. Your hips will not turn near as much, and neither will your feet. Your weight will stay more forward, and "shift" from one leg to the other. In fact, the term "shift" originally comes from the concept of moving all of your weight from one foot to the other. This loads a great deal more power into your punch. A switch shift allows you to open up your opponent to new lines of attack, like a jump shift, but it also lets you load up on power in the same way as stepping through. Without having to travel forwards or backwards.

With A Punch

Example: Dillashaw vs Barao 1 (Dillashaw switches stances with this tactic repeatedly, and even landed a few strikes off of it.)

The Ali Shuffle- Multiple Switch Shifts

Switch Shift Rebound

For the few who can use this technique with any success, it has proved highly valuable. It has the power and distance of a shift, but is faster, and more dynamic. By pushing off of the first foot that lands, you can quickly change angles, opening up new lines of attack and new ways to defensively exit an exchange.

Example: Dillashaw vs Barao 1 – 3ʳᵈ Round (This round is full of TJ using switch shifts as feints as well as him rebounding off of them to land real attacks.)

To rebound off of a Switch Shift, first make sure that both feet become airborne. Shift your weight heavily in one direction. Now push off hard from the first foot that lands, propelling yourself in a new direction.

With Pivot Shuffle Added On

With A Kick

TJ Dillashaw has used this pattern to land a KO with this same kick. You can use the rebound to add distance, pushing off of your new back leg. You can also use it to change angles by either using your new back leg to angle your attack offline, or by using either leg to push off sideways into a neutral stance.

Example: TJ Dillashaw vs
Raphael Assuncao

It is possible to rebound once again off of the first movement, off of the next foot to land. This can create multiple angle changes, one after the other. Transitioning between linear and lateral movement by rebounding is a powerful concept. We will cover these sequences at the end of the book.

Kick Shifts (Check Shifts, Kick Feint Shifts)

A Kick Shift is exactly what it sounds like. It consists of setting your rear leg kick down rather than retracting it back to your on guard position, and switching from orthodox to southpaw or vice versa as you do so.

This technique is commonly used by Max Holloway, who goes about entering exchanges in an very strategic manner. Up into recently, roundhouse kicks were the vast majority of leg kicks being thrown. The circular trajectory and large load up meant that it was somewhat difficult, clumsy, or awkward to enter with these kicks. Furthermore, they are highly telegraphic and any attempt to enter into closer range off of them could easily be countered.

But Holloway will throw rear leg stomp kicks/push kicks/front snap kicks to his opponents leg, and then take a superior position by setting his kicking foot down. The motion of dropping his weight down off of his kick loads up power into his punches. He knocked down Pettis in this exact same way.

Leg Kick Shift Enter

Example: Max Holloway vs Anthony Pettis (Holloway used kicks to enter into many different superior positions and set up a variety of strikes and grappling techniques. He's single handedly advanced striking to an extent few have yet realized.)

Once Holloway has established his kicks as a threat, he will simply feint a kick in order to shift forward aggressively. This acts as a preemptive leg check, negating the risk of those counters.

Knee/Knee Fake Shift Enter

As an additional benefit, the threat of a leg kick sometimes causes the opponent to check, leaving them temporarily immobile. This can let you come in even deeper, setting up move aggressive angles of attack. "Mighty Mouse" Johnson will sometimes use kick shifts to move backward, throwing a lead leg kick and retracting it far back to shift backwards, allowing for a faster escape.

Spin Shift

This technique is mostly used to set up spinning attacks, like spinning back fists or wheel kicks. It can also be used to feint such attacks as well. It would be well advised to throw a jab or feint a hook before committing to a spin attack, or to use spinning attacks as counters only. They are high risk, high reward.

Example: Yoel Romero vs Ronaldo Souza (1ˢᵗ Round Knockdown.)

Turn Shift (Turning to Face Circling Opponent Rather Than Pivot)

This technique is commonly used by multi-stance fighters, like Mike Tyson and Marvin Hagler. As an opponent circles around you, the normal tried-and-true technique is to stay aligned by pivoting, tracking their movements. However, it can be faster at times to merely stay as you are and turn, shifting into a new stance. Think of it like this; If your opponent is circling towards your rear foot, then it may be simpler to just turn, turning your rear foot into your lead foot.

Let The Opponent Circle, Then Turn and Attack

Example: **Hagler vs Willie Monroe 3 KO (Hagler used this technique constantly, and landed several KO's off of it.)**

Many opponents will be taken by complete surprise by this maneuver. Hagler knocked out multiple opponents from this exact setup. Fighting in southpaw, with his right leg forward, Hagler would throw lead jabs and hooks. This encouraged his opponents to circle inside, to Hagler's left. When they did so, Hagler would Turn Shift into an orthodox stance, step forward with his new lead foot, and connect with a lead hook or a cross. This technique is also a great way to better cut off the ring. Tyson would regularly switch into a southpaw stance when his opponent moved to his right, so as to better corner them, and put his right hand closer to his opponent.

Gazelle/Shuffle Turn Shift

Yes, it looks this weird when Tyson does it too, but also terrifying, because... Tyson.

Speaking of Tyson, he had an entirely unique way of throwing his lead hook, and what made it so exceptional was the bizarre footwork involved. Tyson's hook would begin as a gazelle punch (a shuffle into a lead hand strike) but would then take a drastic turn. The insane power of Tyson's lead hook would ensure that the opponents would franticly moved to the inside to avoid it. When they did so, Tyson would shuffle forward, and then Turn Shift mid air. By the time his punch landed, he was in or close to being in a southpaw position. His lead hook had transitioned into a rear hook mid punch. You can watch my video on Tyson if you want to see this in action.

Example: Tyson vs Savarese KD or Tyson vs Mike Jameson KO

D' Amato Shift

Once more, as we examine the more complex footwork, Tyson plays a major part. Tyson's legendary coach, Cus D'Amato, made sure Tyson was comfortable fighting squared up to his opponent, in a Neutral stance. This often resulted in Tyson moving past the centerline, shifting both his stance, AND his opponent's stance at the same time. Comfortable in any position, Tyson was in his element. His opponents were not. They had now been put, unexpectedly, into a position they were not used to fighting in.

<u>Both Fighters Start Off In Orthodox, Then The D' Amato Shift Changes Both to Southpaw</u>

Example: Tyson vs Mark Young KO or Hagler vs Roldan KO (Both Tyson and Hagler were multi-stanced fighters.

76

Today, Demetrious Johnson uses D'Amato Shifts consistently to exit echanges. He usually clinches as he does so, adding an extra layer of security.

Step Through D'Amato Shift

Example: Wonderboy Thompson's finish of Robert Whitaker.

Outside D'Amato Shift

Example: Roy Jones Jr vs James Tony & Roy Jones Jr. vs Hall (Jones Knocked down Hall in the first with this technique, but off of an open stance, even more impressive.)

Example 2: Max Holloway vs Cole Miller Round 2 2:20 Minutes Left (Holloway spun into this attack, adding another lever of complexity.)

Neutral Stance Footwork

Half Shift

A Neutral stance lets you easily move into any position with an equal amount of ease. With both feet even, it is twice as easy to move into most positions, as the distance needed has been halved. The downsides should be obvious. This stance leaves you almost entirely vulnerable. However, transitioning into a Neutral position mid combination, or as a deceptive Entry into an exchange, can be a great way to remain elusive as well as transition between stances with precision and balance.

To Half Shift, Simply Step Your Rear Foot Forward or Your Lead Foot Back

Side Lunge

A side lunge is like a half shift, but instead of moving forward, you lean hard to the side. At the same time, you can either push off to create space, shuffle out, or both. This technique is used by most movement fighters, including Muhammad Ali, Willie Pep, Archie Moore, Dominick Cruz, Demetrious Johnson, TJ Dillashaw, and many, many more.

Side Lunge Left

Side Lunge Right

This Movement Was Called A Side Step In the 1940's classic book *Boxing by Edwin Haislet. Nowadays, a side step simply means a basic step to the side.*

It is primarily used as a quick way to escape. However, some fighters do use this footwork technique to land shots, usually intercepting an opponent as they move forward to attack. Attacks off of this movement will usually lack power, as the body is not properly aligned to deliver force, and your weight will be moving away from the direction of the strike.

82

Landing A Strike Off This Movement Takes Skill

Example: Archie Moore vs Yvon Durelle 1 (Moore used this to slip jabs, while his cross guard kept him safer in his now more squared up position. He did this in every fight, but everyone should see this one, it's incredible.)

Side Lunge With Lateral Shuffle

This is a shuffle used from a Neutral Stance or Parallel Stance to quickly turn back towards your target. Commonly, you will Laterally Shuffle off of a Side Lunge, while turning to strike. It's worth practicing if you want to use the kind of footwork that Dominick Cruz or those like him use, but it feels extremely awkward at first. The hardest part is staying grounded and maintaining balance.

Moving Left

Example: Sean O'Malley vs Andre Soukhamthath Round 2 3:20 Left

Chapter 3: Strategy

Every part of your style should be integrated, part of a larger, coherent whole. From the way you step to the way you plan to progress and finish your fights, every single technique you add to your repertoire should blend in seamlessly with the rest of your style. This is much easier said than done. Most fighters don't develop distinct styles until much later in their careers. However, everyone has some things they are better at than others, and everyone has certain inherent inclinations when the bell rings.

If you already have a generalized or even specific idea about which strategies and tactics you employ, then this chapter should help you fine-tune your style. If you do not, then that's great too. Maybe it will help you get a clearer idea of what your style is or simply help you get a little better at everything. In general, getting anything to work as a coherent whole becomes more and more difficult as the amount of complex parts are increased. This is true from machines, to governments, to fighting styles. Fights are especially chaotic, for obvious reasons. But it is my hope that the categories below will provide a concrete starting point, and give a good idea of how each element of fighting fits together. We will start from a macro level and work our way down to a micro level.

Ring Control

Ring Control is the concept of how well you are able to position yourself and your opponent within the confines of the ring (or Octagon or what have you.) Every single exchange, every feint, every step should be in line with your overarching strategy for controlling the ring. There are many, many strategies when it comes to ring control. Some fighters spend the majority of their fights moving backwards, yet may still win the majority of their fights. Though they may be moving backwards they are still "controlling" the ring by positioning themselves where they would like to be and forcing their opponents to fight their kind of fight. Of course, there are fighters who like to drive their opponents to the ropes or cage, fighters who prefer close range engagements, fighters who like to pick their opponents apart with low risk strikes from long range, and fighters who use footwork primarily to take their opponents to the ground. Even amongst fighters who are primarily grapplers, there are many different variations. For instance, some prefer to take their opponents to the ground directly through explosive takedowns. While others prefer to grab a hold of their opponents and drive them to the cage first. Let's start by taking a look at the most condensed idea possible: Do we want to be moving forward, backwards, or sideways?

Cutting Off The Ring

Pressure fighters use their power and/or high work rate to intimidate their opponents and back them against the ropes or cage. For mixed martial artists, this can be used to clinch and take the fight to the ground. For boxers or kickboxers, it is a way to eliminate the potential for movement. When pressuring an opponent, it is usually best to move diagonally to cut off the ring. This ensures that the opponent cannot escape by moving laterally.

There are two ways to do this. The first is to widen your stance as you move, stepping laterally. This will leave you more open, as the more lateral steps will square up your body. However, your rear leg will be in a better position to enter an exchange, especially if you are comfortable shifting forward. Watch GGG to see how to catch opponents by shifting forward at an angle just as they try to escape the corner.

Step Out Wide To Cut Off The Ring And Aid Lateral Movement

Another way is to cross step your lead foot in front of your back. This keeps you more sideways, allowing for more protection and better linear movement. Once again, GGG is a great example.

Cross Step To Stay Defensive And Aid Linear Movement

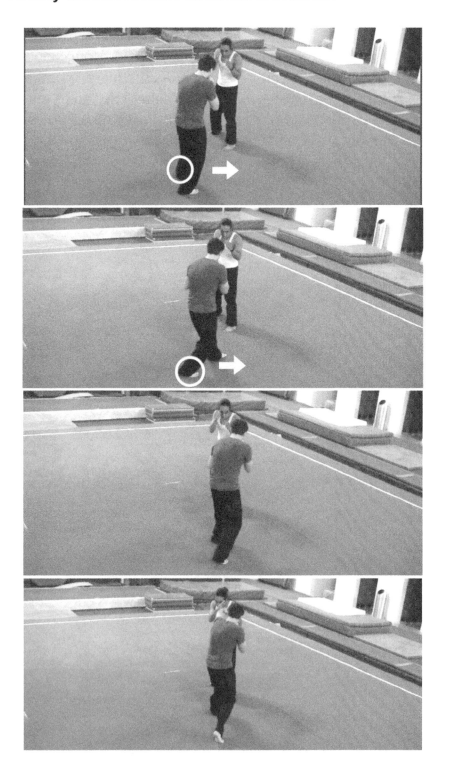

You can also shift or turn shift, positioning your lead hand and foot closer to attack and using your body as an obstacle so that your opponent cannot escape. Tyson is a great example of this tactic.

Shifting Is A Major Benefit When Cutting Off The Ring

The last technique is to simply come straight at your opponent. This is highly dangerous, and you need something outside of good footwork to make this work. Frazier got away with it through superb head movement, Foreman through guard manipulation, and Khabib through a mixture of head movement and grappling.

Escaping The Ropes: Exiting Outside

While it's possible to escape the ropes by simply gritting your teeth and taking some shots, or through grappling, neither of these is what this book is about. Let's take a look at how to escape the ropes through footwork, and then, look at how to stop an opponent from doing so.

There are two options when escaping the ropes. You can either Exit Outside, circling towards your opponent's back, or Exit Inside, towards your opponents front. Escaping Outside is usually preferable, as you will be moving towards your opponent's weaker hand and foot. There are some exceptions to this, of course. No one wanted to move towards Tyson's or Frazier lead hand, as their Lead Hooks were devastating. That being said, it is usually the safer method.

Keeping The Opponent Trapped Against the Ropes/Cage: Opponent Attempts Outside Exit

To trap an opponent against the ropes in boxing almost necessitates widening your stance and using lateral movement. Trapping them in the corner requires the least amount of movement to keep them trapped. This is not so in kickboxing and MMA. Here, you can remain more sideways (and therefore relatively safer) by throwing spinning attacks off of your Rear Side to intercept an opponent as they try to leave.

<u>Lateral Movement</u>

Example: Gaethje vs Vick KO

Fighter 2 (White Shirt) Attempts to Move Outside To Escape Being Driven To The Cage.

On the Left Side Picture, Fighter 1 (Grey Shirt) Steps Laterally, widening his stance to land a Long Hook. In the Right Side Picture, Fighter 1 employs a Lead Leg Round Kick to the stomach to do the same. Both examples necessitate Fighter 1 to open his stance.

With Spin Attacks

Example: McGregor vs Brandao

Once again, Fighter 2 tries to move Outside to regain the center of the ring.

This time, Fighter 1 stays in a more bladed, sideways stance, and drives Fighter 2 into his Wheel Kick.

Keep in mind, this must be done at a longer range to work. There is always just as much risk when spinning at close range as when opening up your stance with lateral movement. Still, it is a great option for In/Out fighters with sideways stances. This technique can even be employed with the opponent attempting to exit to the Inside. Simply Jump Turn (See Chapter 2) to quickly switch stances and throw a spin kick from your new back leg. If this sounds overly fancy, it is, but it also works. Sugar Sean O'Malley just pulled it off in his last fight.

Escaping The Ropes: Exiting Inside

This is technically more dangerous, since you are moving towards your opponent's "Power Side." In other words, you are moving towards their rear hand and foot, which they can usually hit harder with. However, the fact that their rear hand and foot have longer to travel does give you some extra time and room to escape.

Keeping The Opponent Trapped Against the Ropes/Cage: Opponent Attempts Inside Exit

<u>**With Shifting**</u>

Example: GGG has scored multiple KO's this way, and Tyson vs Eddie Richardson is another great example of using this technique to end a fight.

Fighter 2 attempts to circle Inside, towards Fighter 1's Power Side.

Fighter 1 Steps in and throws an Overhand, then slides his Rear Leg Forward to cut off Fighter 2's escape route.

Fighter 1 then throws a Rear Hook from Open Stance and drives Fighter 2 further into the corner with a Lead Leg Roundhouse Kick.

Staying Mid Ring/Octagon

While most fighters are happy to back an opponent into the rope or cage when they feel they are near finished, many choose not to do so from the beginning. Rather than rely on work rate, aggression or fire power to overwhelm their opponents, they instead choose to fight in the center of the ring. This way, they can take advantage of the additional space to cut angles, counter attacks, and avoid the inherent damage that comes with pressing forward. These fighters have developed a number of techniques to stay at their preferred location and range.

The first is to circle. This forces the opponent to constantly turn and readjust. Circling inside is often the preferred choice when in a closed stance with your opponent, as you have access to more targets. However, it does move you closer to their rear arm and leg, making it more likely that you get caught with a strike from their power side. The trick is stay one step ahead, only attacking at the right time, moving in slightly faster than they can turn, so that they remain unbalanced.

Circling Inside

Example: Ali vs Williams

Circling Outside

Circling outside in a closed stance is safer, but more difficult from a kinetic standpoint. It also allows for less targets within range of the strikes from you power side.

Example: Holloway vs Aldo 1 (Holloway circled outside to negate the risk of Aldo's legendary leg kicks.

Circling Outside In An Open Stance

In an open stance, these concepts are reversed. You are in a much better position to circle outside, establishing lead foot dominance.

Example: Lomachenko vs Linares

Circling Inside In An Open Stance

But circling inside can still be useful to maintain distance by establishing your jab, and puts a fighter at a great angle to counter an opponent's rear limb attacks.

Example: Manny Pacquiao circles inside to remain defensive after exiting an exchange.

Mid ring/cage fighters can also maintain distance with linear, in and out attacks. This requires great timing and distance management. In MMA and kickboxing, this can be done by quickly stepping in with sidekicks, round kicks or oblique kicks to the lead leg; or sidekicks and teeps to the body. Jabs and check hooks work well too and are the primary distance keepers in boxing.

Maintaining Distance Using Non-Telegraphic Footwork To Set Up Linear Attacks

Fighter 1 uses Pendulum Steps and Half Steps to confuse Fighter 2 as to his true intentions.

Example: McGregor uses a non-telegraphic sidekicks off of pendulum steps to keep his opponents at range in every fight.

Fighter 1 then comes in with a Lead Leg Side Kick to the knee. It lands, because Fighter 2 could not distinguish Fighter 1's footwork from a real attack. Fighter 2 will be wary of Fighter 1's Feints and Preparatory Movements from now on, allowing Fighter 1 to control distance without attacking.

Intercepting An Opponent's Attack

As well as manipulating your own timing, you can learn to better read your opponents. This will allow you to intercept him easily, helping you to maintain distance.

Fighter 1 lands an Oblique Kick and parries Fighter 2's Jab. Jon Jones often employed this technique, but 50 years before he did, Bruce Lee was demonstrating it at seminars.

Teeps and Sidekicks to the stomach work equally well.

The last effective way to stay mid ring is to maneuver past and around your opponent, using extreme Lateral and Parallel Movement. This is much easier said than done. Dominick Cruz, "Mighty Mouse" Johnson, and Willie Pep are the best practitioners of these techniques in the history of combat sports.

When throwing or intercepting an attack, they will often end up behind their opponent at the end of the exchange. Many times this tactic eliminates the need to circle. The fighter can have their back against the ropes/cage one second, and be standing dead center in the middle of the ring the next.

Cutting Angles To Regain The Center Of The Ring/Cage

The Same Technique With Guard Manipulation (Used By Demetirious Johnson)

Johnson will grab one of his opponents wrists and Arm Drag him off balance as he D' Amoto Shifts off of the ropes. Absolutely insane.

Trapping Mobility Fighters

We've already covered a few ways to corner opponents and cut off the ring, and we will cover more later in this chapter, and again with individual combinations in Chapter 5. However, there is one unique trick that is well worth mentioning that was used prevalently by Floyd Mayweather, and more recently by Tyron Woodley. These fighters will put THEMSELVES against the ropes. This seems crazy at first, but you only have to watch Woodley vs Thompson or Mayweather vs... pretty much anybody later in his career, to see that it works. The question is, how?

Certain fighters are so used to certain angles that they do terribly when they are taken away from them. When Mayweather takes himself to the corner, he is essentially shortening and tightening both himself and the opponent's ability to move. He's creating an environment where he knows he will thrive. The Philly Shell guard is ideal for taking tighter angles and beating the opponent to the punch. And while his opponent has no other way to Exit Exchanges than by going straight back, Mayweather has multiple Exits available to him. All of which leave him behind his opponent in a Superior Position. Woodley has adapted this and added on explosive Takedown and an incredible Rear Hand. This is definitely not a strategy for everybody, but it's well worth mentioning.

The 4 Transitions

Condensed down as much as possible, there are 4 phases of combat, each of which transitions and builds upon the others.

1 - Preparatory Patterns

2 - Entry

3 - Adjustments

4 - Exit

1 - Preparatory Patterns

Preparatory Patterns

Preparatory Patterns are footwork and body movement patterns used to prepare for exchanges. They vary from feints, in that they are not meant to trick the opponent into thinking an attack is coming. (However, they can be used in conjunction with feints.) Instead, they are used to aid specific movements.

Before going more in depth, we will start with an example. One of the best and most succinct examples of using Preparatory Patterns recently might be the recent twenty second fight between Marlon Moraes and Jimmie Rivera. Moraes first Half Stepped in and back with a Foot Feint at kicking range. A few seconds later, he came in the exact same way, but this time, landed a leg kick off of the pattern.

Next, Moraes executed a Pendulum Half Shift, drawing his lead leg back until he was in a Neutral Stance. He then stepped back into position and continued circling. A few seconds later, Moraes executed that same pattern again, but this time, he attacked off of the movement, knocking Moraes out off of a left leg kick from a Neutral Stance.
It's easy to see what happened. Moraes used preparatory movements that mimicked the attacks he was about to throw. There are several reasons why this works so well, and why all high-level fighters use Preparatory Movements.

Preparatory Movements Ease Entry Into Exchanges

Preparatory Movements dull your opponent's reaction to Entries by getting them used to certain patterns and movements. For example, Pendulum Steps will disguise almost any attack that requires a step forward or backwards. The constant in and out movement of the lead foot gets the opponent used to your lead leg moving in, making it difficult to determine if a step forward will lead to an attack or not. Similarly, bouncing your rear foot inside and back to slightly square up your body will dull your opponent's reaction to rear leg attacks by getting them used to the seeing the beginning motion of those attacks. There are many, many more examples.

Willie Pep's C-Steps and back and forth lateral movement disguised his intentions, allowing him to set traps and drive opponents into his punches as they chased him right into an incoming blow. TJ Dillashaw's constant Pendulum Steps help disguise his Switch Shifts. Also, by mimicking the beginnings of your attacks, you can gauge your opponent's reactions to them, getting a good feel for their speed, and if they are over or under reactive.

Upper body movement can be used in much the same way, mimicking the start of punches, while also keeping you safe by constantly moving your head. Which brings us to the next function of preparatory movement, defense.

Preparatory Movements Aid Defense

Preparatory Movements should facilitate footwork patterns with multiple purposes, not only offensive movements. The movements should also aid with lateral and backwards motion. An object in motion tends to stay in motion, and the more you are already moving, the easier it will be to keep moving. Staying with the example of the Pendulum Step, the in and out movement allows for a smooth transition into L Steps, or any kind of shuffle really.

Examples

The most common Preparatory Movement is a Pendulum Step. Begin by circling to the inside, stepping and pivoting. Now, every few steps, add in a couple Pendulum Steps. Now, intermittently throw in some L-Steps when drawing your leg back from the Pendulum Step. Once you have that down, add on some push steps into a jab and pivot out. Finally, add in some Foot Feints by adding Half Steps off of your Pendulum Steps, randomly alternating your Foot Feints with real Steps and jabs.

As mentioned before, Preparatory Footwork should absolutely be mixed with upper body movements and striking feints for maximum effectiveness.

2 - Entry

Broken Rhythm

Rhythm is the ability to move throughout your techniques with consistent, steady, and smooth timing. When a fighter first learns a new technique, or tries to put certain techniques together, there may be awkward pauses and breaks in rhythm. Over time, as the techniques become integrated, the fighter manages to move smoothly, with perfect balance, even during combat. Developing this ability is incredibly difficult, as your opponent will do everything in their power to keep you guessing while attempting to unbalance you and throw off your timing.

The minute adjustments necessary to maintain rhythm and balance against an unpredictable opponent take years to develop, even after the technique and patterns have been fully mastered on the bag, pads, and during shadow boxing. Only sparring is adequate to fully develop your skills.

Smooth, consistent rhythm is important, but it is equally important to be able to break it at will. During your preparatory patterns, feints, or even during mid exchange, breaking your rhythm can be highly beneficial. You can do this by suddenly and rapidly increasing your speed, or by pausing for a split second before coming in with your real attack. This will keep you unpredictable. If you want to see an example in striking, watch Mayweather's jab in his fight against Canelo.

In footwork, broken rhythm is used to trick opponents about where and when you will attack. Some examples of this are detailed below.

Foot Feints

Foot Feints are when you make your opponent react to the idea of you moving to a position that you do not intend to move, or have not moved to yet.

Probably the best fighter to watch to get a hold of this is Sugar Ray Leonard. Leonard's feet were incredibly fast, and many times he didn't bother to feint his jab, or even throw it, before coming in with his cross. He would simply vary how many steps he took to get into position before throwing his cross or unloading his right hand. Sometimes he would take one step in, sometimes two, sometimes three. Half of the time, he would step back out of range, having never thrown a punch. The other half, he would come in fully committed.

This was all done on a near straight line (He did circle a great deal, I am only referencing this specific technique), but you can also foot feint laterally, stepping left before breaking right, or stepping right to rebound left.

Drawing

Drawing means tempting your opponent into throwing strikes or takedowns so you can counter them. Good counter-punchers can draw an attack and then run their opponent right into their strike, as they know exactly where their opponent is about to be.

To do this you need lightning fast reflexes and superb balance. You need to step in deep enough to convince your opponent you are open to attack, but stay light enough to quickly move out of harm's way before returning with your own shot.

GSP is probably the best fighter to watch to learn about drawing. GSP has a magnificent jab (compliments of Freddie Roach), and he'll use it to draw aggressive attacks from his competitors. Half the time he will pivot out of his jab, staying at a safe distance. But the other half, he will perform reactive takedowns, using his opponent's own attacks against them. By striking, your opponents shift their balance, leaving them vulnerable to takedowns.

Short Stop

In the same way you can trick an opponent into overreaching with their strikes, you can also trick them into overreaching with their footwork.

By getting your opponent used to chasing you, you can condition them to aggressively follow in a certain direction. You can then stop short, allowing them to move past a position of safety, and drive your own attack home.

Manny Pacquiao has done this consistently throughout his boxing career.

In MMA, there is no better example of this than Jon Jones' dismantlement of Daniel Cormier. Jones would circle away from DC at a consistent rhythm before stopping short while DC was still mid step. DC would continue moving in the same direction, while Jones moved in at a superior angle to take advantage of the openings.

Trick Your Opponent Into Overstepping Laterally

Example: Jon Jones vs Daniel Cormier 2 (Jones used this technique repeatedly during the last round of the fight.)

Fighter 1 backs away, moving to the Inside. Fighter 2 follows.

Fighter 2 over-commits to his Step. Before Fighter 2 puts his foot down, Fighter 1 has begins to Step Outside, to gain a Superior Angle.

By the time Fighter 2's Lead Foot Lands, Fighter 1 has taken an Outside Position.

Fighter 1 now drives a hook into Fighter 2's stomach. This is an exact sequence form Jones vs Cormier 2.

A more simplistic version of this technique would be the way Barboza lands his spinning wheel kicks. He suddenly stops moving backwards and plants down as his opponents continue to chase him. He then throws his wheel kick before they have a chance to react.

Short Stop Moving Backwards

Example: Edson Barboza vs Terry Etim KO

Fighter 1 retreats, and Fighter 2 chases.

Fighter 2 has over-committed, and fighter one lands a Spinning Wheel Kick

Lateral Entries With Linear Strikes & Vice Versa

Despite all of the advantages in mobility that fighters like Willie Pep or Dominick Cruz enjoy, it is worth noting that they can lack in power. This is because the direction in which their body is moving does not always line up with the direction in which their strike is travelling. Dempsey calls this an "impure punch." To him, a "pure punch" was a punch that travelled in the same direction as the rest of your body. All the weight was aligned and moving into the strike. When you move right, punching throwing a hook with your right hand, you dispel a great deal of potential power.

An "Impure" Punch Will Lack Power

Cruz has landed this bizarre punch with this same bizarre body and head movement effectively several times, but it can lack power by its very nature.

Fighters like Lomachenko and TJ Dillashaw use lateral movement to create angles, but then come in linearly, aligning their strikes with their movement. It is a personal choice whether or not you want to use either of these tactics, but it is something worth noting.

Final Thoughts

Make sure to vary your rhythm, and occasionally break it, to keep the enemy guessing. In the same way that you should not continue for too long in an established rhythm, you should avoid using the same pattern in the same order repeatedly. If you do, your patterns and your timing can be picked up by your opponent, who will be able to pertain when your attacks are coming. Be careful not to have your preparatory movements become consistent tells for you opponent to pick up on. Variety is key. Do not become predictable in your timing or in your patterns. Each pattern should be capable of having multiple attacks thrown off of it, and you should be able to throw from many different moments in the pattern itself.

The time to practice this is when shadow boxing and hitting the bags. Broken rhythm and unpredictable patterns should become naturally ingrained in your style, and should eventually reach a point where it requires almost no though.

3 - Adjustments

Adjustments are the alterations in position made mid Exchange. They often determine the skill of a fighter, and can win or lose the fight, regardless of what variety of fighters they may be. Unless you are Exiting immediately after throwing the first one or two strikes (Which is a worthwhile and viable option, but often not sustainable) then you will need to give a lot of thoughts about what adjustments to make to stay effective, both offensively and defensively.

As a general rule, your Entry should set up and support your Adjustments. You are essentially building a trap for you enemy to fall into. If you have a good game plan, style, and overall strategy, then this should happen automatically during a fight, with no need to think about it beyond strategic adjustments given by your corner.

Superior Positions

A superior position is one in which you are able to attack your opponent far more easily than they are able to attack you. This relies not only on foot position, but on the angle at which your opponent's body is positioned as well. We will cover these positions in Chapter 4.

Most superior positions will only be available for a split second, as your opponent attempts to adjust.

Maintain Superior Angle Outside

This technique is best used when fighting in an Open Stance, but can be done effectively with a Closed Stance as well. When the opponent stands still, whether attacking or shelling up, it is the perfect moment to change angles, moving outside towards their back. From this position, they must turn in order to reposition themselves to defend or attack. This is why the Outside Position is often called the opponents weak side. In boxing, this gives you valuable time to land attacks while the opponent is still turning. You can continue moving Outside to maintain your position, always staying one step ahead. This tactic is a favorite of Lomachenko.

In MMA, you have more available options, such as securing a body lock, but there are also more dangers. Your opponents are now allowed spinning attacks, including elbows. Still, if set up well, it is a very useful technique. Max Holloway is a great example of a fighter who uses this tactic. He will often even shift into the position off of a kick.

From Closed Position

Example: Henry Armstrong (Any fight.)

Fighter 1 Steps Outside off of his initial attack, maintaining a Superior Angle Outside.

From Open Position

Example: Max Hollaway vs Miller or Mighty Mouse vs Wilson Reis. (Best to watch these sequences in slow motion.)

Fighter 1 pins Fighter 2's arm off of his Jab and Steps and Pivots Outside to a Superior Angle.

Fighter 1 gains Wrist Control and Arm Drags Fighter 2 Inside as he Steps Outside, landing a Hook to Fighter 2's open head.

Fighter 1 now Pivot Shuffles even further Outside. Max Holloway and Demetrius Johnson are using these grappling techniques with advanced footwork.

Maintain Superior Angle Inside

This is second in terms of safety to the Outside Angle, but also allows for more varied kinds of attacks, especially in competitions that limit kicking or grappling. The ideal situation is that your opponent is still facing forwards, towards where you WERE, instead of where you now ARE. However, if they do turn towards you, they will still be wide open while you, being more sideways, are comparatively more safe at a distance. Get too close up though, and your opponent may have an advantage, as your linear punches may be jammed, while their more forward stance is ideal for close range weapons like hooks and elbows.

<u>Closed Position</u>

Example: Sugar Ray Robinson (Any Fight)

Fighter 1 Pivots off of his Jab to stay safe and force Fighter 2 to turn.

Open Position

Example: Manny Pacquiao (Any Fight)

Fighter 1 Steps Inside off of his Cross and throws a Long Hook to stay safe and force Fighter 2 to turn.

Take Aggressive Angle Inside

Aggressive counter punchers like Tyson look to draw punches by forcing their opponents into uncomfortable positions. As a result, their opponents often throw sloppy punches with poor defense, making it all the easier to counter. This is a very risky tactic, as both yourself and your opponent are wide open. Ideally, you should still be more balanced and one step ahead, having surprised your competitor by initiating the position.

Parallel Position

Example: Mike Tyson (Any Fight)

Drive The Opponent Into An Attack

The idea here is to force your opponent to retreat in the direction that you want them to, so you can catch them with a takedown or powerful attack. One way to do this is to throw a powerful lead attack to encourage them to move inside. You then catch them by shifting forward and catching them with your rear hand or foot.

Lead Attack Drives Opponent Into Power Hand

Example: Marvin Hagler (Any Fight)

Lead Attack Drives Opponent Into Power Leg

Example: Jose Aldo (Any Fight)

Conversely, you can use your "power hand" or foot to drive your opponents inside, and then catch them with your lead. This was a favorite of Rocky Marciano and Roberto Duran. The opponents centerline should be wide open, and they should be moving into the force or your blow. Good options are lead hooks or uppercuts, as preferred by Duran, Marciano and Tyson, or lead roundhouse kicks to the midsection or liver, as preferred by Bas Rutten.

Rear Attack Moves Opponent Into Lead Side Attack

Example: Roberto Duran
(Any Fight)

Lead Hand Attack Moves Opponent Into Power Side In Open Stance

Example: Mirko Cro Cop
(Any Fight)

4 - Exit

You should always have an escape plan. In fact, you should have multiple. There is a consistent trend of pressure fighters who get rocked once and then do not know how to respond. Often they will keep moving forward rather than allow themselves to recover. So yes, even pressure fighters should know how to Exit backwards. However, keep in mind that Exits also occur when an opponent leaves the exchange, and pressure fighters should definitely know how to deal with that scenario as well.

Exits should reflect your strategy. Someone looking to catch their opponent at close range and cut off the ring should choose footwork that allows them to stay close and follow their opponent as they attempt to Exit the exchange, hopefully cutting off the ring as they do so. On the other hand, mobility fighters should Exit at an angle that unbalances their opponents, allowing them more time to readjust to a better position. A very very good movement fighter can exit with a D'Amato Shift Inside or Outside. Usually though, stepping out of an exchange at a slight angle will suffice to keep you safe, and perhaps even set up a new line of attack.

Why Fighting Is Compared To Chess - Eliminating the Possibilities

In chess, the idea is to trap your opponent's King in a position to where he is in danger, and cannot move out of it without getting taken out by at least one piece on the board. This is inherently the same in fighting. For every direction in which your opponent moves, you should be prepared to respond with the appropriate reaction to discourage that movement. As you eliminate the possibilities, the opponent runs out of options, until they have no choice left but to do what you want them to.

Consider how this may be done with the strategies laid out above.

Say your opponent tries to move forward with a 1-2, but you duck under and move inside, catching him with multiple counters.

He tries to stay at range, tempting you to charge in off-balance so he can counter you. But you circle around him, wearing him down with long range attacks and picking up points.

You attack, and he tries to move away to the inside, so you shift forward and catch him with a power shot or a takedown.

This time he tries to move outside, but you catch him with a spinning back kick.

In these ways, a well-rounded, experienced, and intelligent fighter can beat a bigger, stronger opponent, or even an opponent who specializes in only one area of fighting. Then again, if a fighter is competently defensive in all other areas, creating a stalemate rather than dominating, then they can win by using the techniques in which they specialize. Either way, every scenario must be dealt with in some manner, or the opponent will pick up on the areas in which the fighter is weak and capitalize on them. All fighters must have a game plan which they are able to perfectly execute.

Long Term Strategies

Let's take a look at some important questions to ask before planning out your overall strategy. Even though every question does not exclusively deal with footwork, your footwork must nonetheless support each of you strategies.

What is your prefered distance, and how to you intend to maintain it?

What are your primary defensive tactics?

How do you intend to wear your opponents down?

How do you intend to finish the fight?

Where are you strongest?

Where are you weakest?

How can you increase your strengths?

How can you limit your weaknesses?

Chapter 4: Positions

This chapter covers positions that a fighter may find themselves in relative to their opponent. Each position comes with advantages and disadvantages. Furthermore, each position is beneficial for setting up certain strikes and takedowns, while making it more difficult to use others. Inversely, each position offers different defensive benefits while leaving a fighter open to other strikes.

A successful fighter knows these positions inside and out, and has established a number of patterns to move in between them in order to set up their offense and establish their defense. We will learn the most common, effective patterns as well as more difficult, advanced patterns in a later chapter.

Most fighters are forced to learn these positions intuitively, as footwork is often taught as an afterthought by all but the very best. Sometimes (If not most times) the corrections are not given at all, and are left to the fighter to refine through sparring. This is an unnecessary and painful learning curve.

Because it's important to understand the ups and downs of your position relative to your opponent, and also as a way to map out different footwork patterns in Chapter 5, I've named each of these positions by foot placement and angle.

However, keep in mind that even although these positions are useful to know, it is the concepts behind them that are important. They are merely the means to accomplish a goal, and are classified for the sake of utility. Just like there are a number of hybrid punches in-between an uppercut and a hook, there are many many positions in between the ones outlined below. But it is still important for a fighter to learn a distinct Hook and a distinct Uppercut at the very start, so he understands their purpose if nothing else.

Once you understand the concepts behind the positions and have practiced with repeated repetitions, you can most likely rely on muscle memory and ignore them for good. It may also be beneficial as you go through this chapter to rewatch some of your favorite fights, and watch for the different positions the fighters go through.

Before we get too caught up in the intricacies of the positions, let's look at the most important underlying foundations of their use.

Consolidated into the simplest terms, changing positions relative to your opponent will do one of three things:

1. Open up your opponent to attack while limiting your opponent's ability to attack you.

2. Open up both you and your opponent to attack.

3. Limit your ability to attack, but limit your opponent's ability to attack as well.

Obviously, the first concept, (opening your opponent to attack while remaining safe yourself), is the most preferred. In a purely positional sense, this is most often done by moving inside or outside to square up your opponent while remaining in a more defensive angle yourself. This boils down to the most well known simplification of fighting there is: Hit and don't get hit.

However, it is difficult to land powerful, clean strikes without at least somewhat opening yourself to attack at times as well. That is where the game gets interesting.

Another consideration in regards to positions is how well aligned each of your hands and feet are to any given target. For instance, one position may be highly beneficial for landing with your rear hand down the centerline, but it may also open you up to your opponents lead hand at the same time.

And the last consideration has to do with navigating around your opponents lead foot. If your opponent were in an entirely squared up stance, like a wrestler, than the lead foot would not be a problem. But as most fighters stand with one side further out than the other, it is important to pay close attention to how to move around this obstacle, in order to inhibit your opponents movement, and to not inhibit your own.

Open vs Closed Positions

Closed Stance In Orthodox

Closed Stance In Southpaw

Most matches take place in a closed stance, meaning both fighters have the same foot forward. Usually, two orthodox (Left foot forward) opponents are fighting. However, if two southpaw opponents were to fight each other, they would also be in a closed stance, as they would both have the same foot (Right foot) forward.

Open Stance - Fighter 1 In Orthodox & Fighter 2 In Southpaw

Open Stance - Fighter 1 In Southpaw & Fighter 2 In Orthodox

An open stance is the position two fighters are in when they have the opposite foot of their opponents forward. In other words, when an orthodox fighter (Left foot forward) is fighting a southpaw fighter (Right foot forward.)

There are many different considerations to take into account when fighting in an open stance rather than the more common closed stance. Certain targets with be much easier to hit than others simple due to the change of positions, and footwork patterns will differ greatly.

Some fighters, like Willie Pep or TJ Dillashaw, change between open and closed positions in order to set up strikes from superior positions. This is a highly risky style and not normally encountered. It will most likely not be necessary to learn how to counter these strategies (Although we will cover that in a later section.) It will still be very important to learn how to fight in an open stance, even if you are an orthodox (Left foot forward) fighter, as you will likely encounter a southpaw fighter (Right foot forward) at some point. If you are a southpaw fighter, it is crucial to learn how to fight in an open position, as most of your opponents will be orthodox (Left foot forward) fighters.

Inside vs Outside

It may not sound scientific, but the easiest way to quickly differentiate between the inside and outside is: Moving to the inside is moving towards your opponents belly button. Moving to the outside is moving towards his back. This holds true whether you are in an open or a closed stance. Moving inside squares your opponent up, creating more easily accessible openings. Moving outside is great for angling in certain strikes and for grappling.

<u>Fighter 2 Faces Forward</u>

Fighter 1 Attacks Inside

Fighter 1 Attacks Outside

The Positions

All of these positions will be used to create footwork sequences in a later chapter, referencing real fighters and giving specific instances in fights when they were used. The most useful combinations will also be shown for the many different patterns.

Closed Stance Positions

Closed Stance On Line Position

In this stance, your opponents lead foot is perfectly aligned with your own. This is a fairly defensive position, leaving both yourself and your opponent on equal terms. It is not a superior position for the majority of techniques. Any real advantage in terms of landing strikes will come from the position of your body relative to your opponent. (Whether your shoulders are more squared up, closed, whether you are crouching, ect.) It is an ideal position to attack the opponents leg with a linear kick, such as a sidekick or low teep, as it is perfectly aligned for a kick with little adjustments needed.

However the primary use of this position is to stay safe as you move around at a safe range. Thinking of keeping your lead foot aligned with that of your opponent is a great way to check that you are not putting yourself in unnecessary risk, or letting your opponent sneak into a better position unaware. This position also makes it easy to move your lead foot in either direction, stepping to the inside or the outside, and facilitating easier spinning attacks by negating the need to step inside to turn your hips through. Some fighters do prefer to circle with their lead foot more inside, some outside, however. It depends on your preference for Entries.

Closed Stance Inside Position One - Lead Foot Slightly Inside & Rear Foot Aligned With Opponents Lead

This is the most defensive way to attack an opponent. It slightly opens up both you and your opponent by putting your lead hand and foot in position to better attack their centerline. It also puts your rear hand in line to cross over your opponents jab, but is not deep enough to shoot straight down the center. At kicking range, it sets up your lead leg to kick your opponents lead leg with a roundhouse or teep, and allows some room to throw a teep or roundhouse to the midsection or head. 90 percent of the time, you will pivot inside to leave this position. Your opponent will most likely pivot as well, closing themselves off from your attack. The jab and pivot while circling sequence is probably the most common in fighting. A fighter will fire off a jab, and the opponent will defend by catching, slipping, ducking, etc, and then step and pivot to catch them with return fire. More on that in a later chapter.

The idea behind this position is that your lead foot is positioned only as far inside as needed to accomplish the job. Similarly, if you plan to pivot out of your attack rather than follow up by stepping in deeper, than you should aim to only move in as close as necessary. This will make it easier to exit safely.

But the greatest benefit to this position is that it is a fairly safe way to transition to almost any other position, inside and out. Many fighters use it as the foundation of their style, mixing up several different attacks off of this small step inside.

In boxing, it is used for the jab, body jab, and long hook. In kickboxing, lead leg kicks can be incorporated to help establish distance and set up yet more attacks (GSP being a great example that we will cover later). In MMA it can set you up for a larger, deeper penetrations step for takedowns off of your jab, or help you draw attacks for reactive takedowns.

If there is one thing to remember in particular, it is to only step in as much as necessary the majority of the time. This is the position to establish your distance. If your opponent far out-reaches you, you will need to use head movement or angle deeper inside in order to reach your target. This is far from impossible though, Tyson rarely had a superior reach to his opponents.

Closed Stance Inside Position Two: Lead Foot Inside Far Off Centerline & Rear Foot Inside or Even With Opponents Rear

    This position opens up a line of attack for your rear hand to connect inside. You can also fire harder shots off of your lead hand or foot, as you have more space available to turn into your attacks.

    From kicking range, this position sets up your rear leg to kick your opponent's lead. It gets your head nicely off centerline, making it harder for your opponent to attack you from kicking range. It also lets you leave an exchange easily by shuffling away inside. Roy Jones Jr. would use this position to lead with his rear hand before shuffling out consistently, although that is of course a very dangerous technique.

A good frame of reference is to think of stepping out at a 45 degree angle, but it will vary due to the opponent or the situation. Your rear hand or foot should be close enough to land, but your upper body should be out of harm's way.

This position can leave you open to an opponent's rear hand or leg, but if your lead side is far enough away from his centerline, the power will be dispersed as they overreach. If you are this far away, however, it will be difficult to put any power into your own shot. If you want to get in close enough to generate power, than it is best to not only set up this shot well, but also to have an exit plan. Use good footwork in conjunction with head movement and grappling to exit.

If you are closer to your opponent this position may jam their straight punches, only allowing for hooks or uppers. Going in deep with this position should be avoided if you are uncomfortable fighting with your other foot forward, as it can also lead to unintentionally stance switches, putting your other foot closest to your opponent.

Closed Position Inside Three: Lead Foot & Rear Foot Deep Inside & Perpendicular With Opponent

This positions opens up your opponent while keeping your own stance as bladed as you prefer. It is difficult to get into, and you will usually find yourself here after pivoting off of your lead hook or sidestepping and pivoting to get out of the way of an opponent's attack. This stance is great at long range, setting you up to beat your opponents reach with a number of linear attacks, and leaving them wide open.

However, use this stance at close range at your own risk, as if will stifle your lead hand attacks and allow your opponent the distance to grapple and throw hooks and uppercuts.

The important thing to remember about this position (and most others as well) is that you should only stay in it for the duration of time is takes to throw one or two strikes. Any more and your opponent may regain their wits and you will no longer be one step ahead. YouTube is filled with videos of fighters who got too cocky lying on their backs, making funny faces that are entirely out of their control. Don't be one of those guys if you can help it.

Parallel Inside - Lead Foot Aligned With Opponents Rear & Rear Foot Aligned With Opponents Lead

In this position, you are completely squared up with your opponent. This position is used by fighters who specialize in adjusting angles to surprise their opponents, like Willie Pep, Mike Tyson or Wonderboy Thompson. It is great for lateral movement to transition to a superior angle as your opponent misses.

It is also a great way to transition both you and your opponent from a southpaw stance to an orthodox stance, or vice versa. Simply shuffling out left will leave you and your opponent in southpaw, and shuffling out right will leave you and your opponent in orthodox. This is known as a D' Amato shift, after Tyson and Patterson's famous coach, Cus D'aMato. (I am unsure who coined the term for this technique, but I first saw it used on Lee Wylies Youtube channel, so credit may go to him.)

Tyson employed this stance switching technique in many of his fights. It gained him a major advantage, in that he was comfortable fighting with either foot forward, while his opponent was not. In fact, Tyson is one of the few fighters who could use the Open Position not only as a means to transition between stances and create angles from far or mid range, but to pound and wallup his opponent at close range. In the same way the Neutral position jams your opponent's lead arm at close range, the Open position can crowd your opponents arms, making it hard to throw straight punches. This means that the boxer who specializes in looping punches holds the advantage here at close range, as does the MMA Fighter who specializes in grappling or dirty boxing (clinching while striking).

Despite the numerous benefits, it cannot be stated enough times that this positions is the MOST dangerous out of all positions possible. It takes a lot of experience and unreal defense to stay in it for any length of time. Tyson may be able to stand in place and dodge several punches off of head movement alone, but the common fighter is most likely can't. However, don't let that discourage you. Most often you are the best expert when it comes to yourself and you limits. Only you know how far you can go with practice.

Closed Position Outside One: Lead Foot Inside or Online & Rear Foot Outside Angled Out

This is a great position to attack your opponent's outside. If you can angle out, you will be almost entirely safe. It's also ideal for landing crosses or taking your opponent's back. One of the best uses of the position is that is forces your opponent to turn. This gives you a split second edge, allowing you to catch them as they step back into a more favorable position. Because one foot is Inside and one Out, it can be used to transition seamlessly between the two. The lead hand is within reach to land tight hooks or uppercuts through an opponent's guard, and the rear hand has a clear shot at the head. Because of this, it was an absolute favorite of Henry Armstrong, one of the greatest fighters to ever live.

144

Closed Position Outside Two: Lead Foot & Rear Foot Outside

The position is primarily useful to angle in long range attacks. The opponent's lead foot can get in the way of Inside attacks, but it is ideal for circling to the Outside, staying away from the opponent's power side.

Closed Position Outside Three: Lead Foot Outside & Rear Foot In

It is more likely you will use this as a transition position. This position is primarily useful to set up spin kicks or spin back fists. Joe Frazier would often land his lead hook in this position, but he was able to immediately pivot outside to face his opponent once again. Keep in mind that this creates a superior angle for your opponent, so it's best not to stay in it.

Open Stance Positions

Open Online

The same things apply to this stance as to the Closed Online Position. However, an open stance does come with it's own different set of rules that are worth exploring before delving into the other positions. The most important difference is that both fighters are far more vulnerable to being hit by the others rear hand or foot. This is because there is no arm, leg, or shoulder "in the way" to block or obscure your target.

On the other hand, your lead hand and foot being so close to your opponents lead hand and foot may make it more difficult to land with a lead strike. As such, it often becomes far more important to use your lead hand and leg to try and control your opponent's lead hand or leg, rather than use it to strike. This can help to set up an attack by clearing space or trapping your opponent in place, rather than wasting energy on jabs or such. That being said, there have been fighters who excel at jabbing in an open stance, the southpaw boxer Pernell Whitaker being one of them.

Open Stance Inside Position One: Lead & Rear Foot Inside Opponents

This position puts your lead hand and foot closer to your opponents centerline, shortening the distance your punches and kicks needs to travel to reach your opponent's centerline. It is equally effective to step or pivot out of the Inside or the Outside, but distance must be maintained when circling Inside, as it puts you closer to your opponent's power hand and foot (their rear hand and foot.) Circling, stepping, or pivoting outside off of this jab is particularly difficult. If you step in too deep, you can not pivot out without getting tripped up, as you will run right into your opponents lead leg.

You must quickly step in and then slide out as you retreat. Once again, refer to footage of Pernell Whitaker to see how this is done. We will go deeper into this this sequence and many others in a later chapter.

Lastly, this position puts your opponent into a dominant position to land with their power hand. While your lead hand and foot is closer to your opponent's centerline, their rear hand and foot is now closer to your centerline. For this reason it is often taught that this is a weaker position to be in. However, that is not the case.

If you find that your opponent has put their lead foot on the outside of yours, you should be able to easily beat their cross with your jab or angle your hook down, over their guard. This is another reason lead hand control is so important in an open stance. If your lead hand has been trapped or knocked away, there is little you can do to stop an opponent's cross from landing in this position. In the same way that a jab can beat your opponent's cross here, your lead teep, side or back kick can beat their rear leg roundhouse kick or teep, although it may lack power if you do not load it properly. This position also puts your opponent's rear leg in range. Andy Hug would often land a rear leg round kick to his opponent's rear leg off of this same position.

Open Stance Inside Position Two: Lead Foot Deep Inside & Rear Foot Angled In

This position opens up your opponent while keeping your own stance in alignment. This stance is great at long range, setting you up to beat your opponent's reach with a number of linear attacks, leaving them wide open.

Remember to be careful not to get into this stance at close range. Doing so will stifle your lead hand attacks and allow your opponent the distance to throw hooks both Inside and Outside.

This stance is difficult to get into, however. Although it takes perfect timing, it is possible to safely transition to this position to land a cross off a jab from the inside. This gives you an inside position from which to land with your power side in an open stance. It requires you to step deep in and pivot smoothly off of your lead foot. Often, it is easier to get into this position as a reaction to your opponent's movement. We will look touch further on that in the sequences section.

Open Stance Position Inside Three: Lead Foot Deeper Inside Than Rear Foot & Back Turned To Opponent

Usually you'll find yourself in this position after you have made a critical mistake. Your opponent can easily catch you as you turn or take your back. However, this position can help you transition into spinning moves, and that may be the best way to get out of it if you find yourself here by accident.

Open Stance Outside One: Lead Foot Outside & Rear Foot Inside or Neutral

When you hear someone describe two fighters in an open stance having a "lead foot fight" or looking for lead foot dominance, that means that both fighters are trying to obtain this position. That's because it aligns your power hand and foot down the centerline, opening up your opponent to your power blows. Also, with your lead foot outside, it should be relatively easy to exit the exchange safely. Keep in mind that this position does align your opponent's lead hand and foot closer to you. This means that they will have a chance to land first as you square up to throw your power shot from your rear side making lead hand control very important. If you can trick your opponent into checking with their lead leg, that's even better.

This position can set up powerful kicks to the liver, which is apparently one of the most painful experiences a human being can go through. Check out some old Bas Rutten fights for reference.

Open Stance Outside Two: Lead Foot Far Outside & Rear Foot In or Neutral

This position is great for landing long range, clipping shots. Overhands to the head, looping hooks to the body or rear leg roundhouse kicks to the leg are all great options. This position is often used to lead with the rear hand. Wonderboy Thompson and Dominick Cruz do so today, and Roy Jones Jr. did so in the past.

Open Stance Outside Three: Lead Foot Outside & Rear Foot Outside Angled Out

This is the position Lomachenko is famous for. It exposes your opponent almost entirely, forcing them to turn or continue to get beaten on. As they do turn, you have plenty of time to land your shots, or lock their backs. This position requires a lot of skill to get to, and your opponent will try everything they can to stop you from achieving it. You must have fast feet. It also doesn't hurt to get your opponent immobile first, by tempting them to shell up or by leg checking.

Neutral Positions

These positions are great for lateral movement. On the outside, that means bouncing back and forth to keep your opponent guessing, or circling as quickly as possible. Once again, Pep and Cruz are the absolute best example of this technique. The idea is to quickly dart out of the way of your opponent's attack and come back at a superior angle, or to move diagonally to attack with either foot forward. This position is very much preferred by movement based fighters.

This stance has its uses at midrange as well. It's great for fluidly transitioning between the Inside and Outside, and Closed and Open Positions. Lomachenko will often move into this position before shuffling Inside to switch into an Orthodox stance, before then reversing the process.

On the Inside, it's a great way to crowd your opponent's lead hand and connect with hooks from either side. This was a favorite of Tyson.

A Neutral Position deeper Inside will not only allow you to move laterally, but Parallel to your opponent as well, adding D'Amato shifts to the wide range of positions you can transfer into. A Neutral Position closer to the Outside allows for Outside D'Amato Shifts.

As always, an increase in mobility comes with certain liabilities. You need fast feet and phenomenal head movement to heavily rely on these positions. Most fighters can pull it off mid combination, however.

Inside Neutral Position

Outside Neutral Position

Parallel Outside - Lead Foot Aligned With Opponents Lead & Rear Foot Aligned With Opponents Rear

Additional Considerations

Keep in mind that although these positions can provide major advantages, they are not absolute. Some fighters can land a variety of strikes or takedowns from positions that are seemingly impossible. These fighters are gifted athletes, and even so, many of them end up in the "correct" positions after slipping or throwing, as they've unbalanced themselves so much that they need to step to regain their balance. A good example is Ruddock's "Smash Punch."

To throw it, he would unbalance himself by leaning far Inside. The shot would land, despite the fact he had not stepped inside, but had used upper body movement to get the correct angle. After his punch connected, he would usually have to step inside to regain his balance. Yoel Romero did something similar with his KO of Rockhold, sneaking his cross over Rockhold's hook rather than step inside or cross over from the outside. This left him far out of position, crashing into Rockhold. But, of course, his poor ending position didn't matter, he had already finished the fight. Ali and Prince Naseem tended to do the same thing in different ways. Manny got KO'd by a punch that by all means had no right to land, but still did.

But these examples are extremely rare, and learning the correct footwork will let you know when and how to substitute footwork for upper body movement, if you are one of the gifted fighters capable of such things.

Lastly, the positions listed are the ideals. They should be practiced in drills and mitts as shown, but like all elements of fighting, it feels entirely different in actual combat. You will be up against someone who does not want to be exposed and who simultaneously wishes to expose you. That is why feints, head movement, and all other elements of fighting must work together to obtain these positions. Even then the truly superior positions will most likely only be available for a split second before your opponent readjusts. However, you should strive to only be in the riskier positions for an instant anyways. We will cover the best ways to move in and out of these positions in chapter 5.

Chapter 5: Basic To Advanced Footwork Sequences

Basic Sequences

Although the advanced section is more exciting, mastering the sequences from this chapter is far more important. They make up the foundations of movement for all great fighters, past and present. Only move onto the intermediate and advanced section to supplement and enhance these sequences.

Closed Stance Sequences

Fighting should rarely be done in a straight line. Linear movement is important, but it must be done in conjunction with movement to the Inside or the Outside. These lateral movements do not need to be dramatic by any means. In fact, in the same way that an experienced fighter can make an opponent miss by less than an inch to gain an advantage, so too can a master of footwork use the very minimal adjustment necessary to achieve the desired result. For these basic sequences, minute adjustments are just as important as aggression.

Pattern 1

- Closed Online To Closed Inside 1 Position Exit by Pivoting

The point of attaining the inside position is to open up your opponent, squaring him up to your attacks. The choice to be made is how much you wish to square up and open yourself to attacks in the process. Opening up more may lend more power to your attacks and lends the potential for more adjustments. However, it also leaves you in a worse position defensively.

Pattern 1 is the basis of most early, range finding attacks. This is because it opens the opponent to long range attacks while remaining as defensive as possible; while still being effective. It offers several easy routes for escape, from pivoting out of your strike to simply stepping back, and requires little commitment. While it is a low risk, low reward technique, it can be thought of as a launching pad to move in almost any different direction upon completion, as the following patterns will show. From the Closed Inside 1 Position, you are close enough to follow up with an attack to the inside or the outside, but safe enough to exit if your position becomes unfavorable. =

If executed correctly, and with a little variety thrown in, this sequence can be used almost exclusively to wear an opponent down to the point where they can be easily hit with more powerful shots. It's great for counter punchers, as the opponent often become frustrated over time, and begins to overreach with their attacks. If they do not, you can simply win several rounds by outpointing them. Watch Sugar Ray Robinson to study this pattern in motion.

The main strikes to throw off of this slight step inside (Closed Inside Position 1) and Pivot are jabs (with the occasional lead hook for good measure,) lead leg roundhouse kicks to the opponents lead leg, and teeps to the solar plexus.

Jab Example
Step Inside To Open Up Opponent, Jab, Pivot Offline

Example: Any Boxing Match

Both fighters are On Line, neither holding an advantage.

(Above) Fighter 1 steps inside just enough to split Fighter 2's guard. If he has timed his shot correctly, Fighter 2's balance will be disrupted, making for easier follow up shots.

Fighter 1 Pivots off his Jab to narrow his stance, eliminating the temporary openings caused by his attack. From here, he can move deeper inside, Pivot Outside, or step back to exit. Fighter 2 will usually Pivot Inside as well in an attempt to remain defensive.

If Fighter 2 has been taken by surprise and remains open, Fighter 1 may wish to press his advantage.

Remain cautious about moving deeper inside just because your opponent remains squared up. Archie Moore would use this as a trap, letting his opponents circle in deeper so that he could step out and catch them with a hard right.

Pattern 2

- Closed On Line To Closed Inside 1 To Closed Inside 2

Remember, angles are crucial. Almost any position can be advantageous to your opponent if they are able to remain balanced. This usually occurs when you have been read, and your opponent sees your attack coming from a mile away. Ideally, you should always stay one step ahead of your competitor. If they are able to reposition themselves back to a safe angle, then your attack is pointless. Worse yet, they can counter you as you come in, increasing the power of their strike.

That is why you must always vary up your attacks. This is even more important than having good Feints and Preparatory movement. The next several patterns are built off of Pattern 1, the Circle and Jab/Kick. The idea behind Pattern 2 is to step out at a wide angle, squaring yourself up and aligning your rear side attacks with your opponents. It is a highly aggressive (but not *the* most aggressive) pattern, used to set up power shots.

<u>Pattern 2 Rear Hand Example</u>

(Above) Both Fighters are On Line, with neither holding an advantage.

Example: Liddell vs Overeem (Liddell Rocked Overeem with an overhand from this position before finishing him.)

Fighter 1 Steps in with a Jab to Draw a counter.

Fighter 2 takes the bait, and throws a cross. Fighter 1 Slips and Ducks inside, landing his own rear hand.

Exits

Example: Rose Namajunas vs Joanna Jerdzejczyk (Keep in mind that this is a better idea in boxing. Rose paid for putting her lead leg close to Joanna's rear leg repeatedly, taking a number of leg kick counters throughout the fight.)

Pivoting out to Closed Inside 3 Position is a great Exit to this sequence. Fighter 1 is able to leave a parting shot as he Exits off angle, forcing Fighter 2 to reposition himself before attempting another attack. A D' Amato shift is another great Exit, used by Muhammad Ali and Roy Jones Jr.

Pattern 2 Rear Leg Example

Example: Jose Aldo vs Urijah Faber (A brutal example of how to set up leg kicks and remain defensive while doing so.)

(Above) Both Fighters are Online, with neither holding an advantage.

Fighter 1 Steps Inside to Jab, but Fighter 2 successfully parries the Jab, and then Steps and Pivots to find an angle to land his own attack.

In response, Fighter 1 steps deeper Inside to remain safe, and punishes Fighter 2 for Stepping Inside by driving a Roundhouse Kick into his leg. Refer back to the Adjustment section in Chapter 3 for more on how to drive opponents into attacks.

Pattern 3

Online to Inside 1 to Outside 1

I mentioned before that the first several patterns would be predicated off of Pattern 1, and this Pattern is no different. With enough long range strikes to the inside (Pattern 1) your opponent may become conditioned to Side Step or Pivot Inside to avoid your attacks. As they do, you catch them by moving Outside as the move Inside to avoid your first attack. This pattern is especially effective if your opponent is circling Outside anyways, perhaps to try to avoid your rear hand or foot. As your opponent circles away, Step Inside, then Pivot hard off your lead foot or Step out Laterally to put your rear foot into position. This should allow you the reach to catch them.

Counter Off Opponent's Jab

(Above) Fighter 1 Steps Inside to Jab, but Fighter 2 Blocks.

Fighter 2 Pivots Inside and returns fire. Fighter 1 Side Steps, Slipping his Jab.

Fighter 1 runs Fighter 2 into his cross, and blocks off his Exit by cutting him off.

Small Adjustment

Example : Floyd Mayweather Jr. vs Aturo Gatti (Mayweather pivoted off his cross to take an outside position and landed beautiful combinations from this angle.

(Above) Fighter 1 and Fighter 2 are Online, with neither holding a Superior Position.

Fighter 1 Steps Inside, and Fighter 2 Blocks. Fighter 2 is expecting Fighter 1 to enter deeper Inside, but Fighter 1 subtly Pivots off of his Lead Foot to land a Cross on the Outside of Fighter 2's jaw.

Small Angle Cut

(Above) Fighter 1 and Fighter 2 are Online.

Fighter 1 Steps Inside and then Rebounds off his Lead Foot to cut across with a long Lead Hook.

Fighter 1 takes advantage of the new angle created and throws a Cross.

Pattern 4 - Online to Inside 1 To Inside 3

This is a great way to work your way inside, forcing your opponent to respond. As always, the idea is to always stay one step ahead. Remember that your level of success is dependent on your opponent catching up to you. If they can anticipate your attack, then they can catch you with either hand as you enter. The first strike should cause enough damage or loss of balance to warrant the follow up. Or, you can slip, duck, or feint your way inside. But remember, the success of this Pattern is dependent of your first move.

<u>Double Jab</u>

(Above) Fighters are Online

Fighter 1 Steps into Closed Inside 1 Position to Jab.

Fighter 1 Pivots Inside, Fighter 2 Parries, but opens himself to another attack.

Fighter 2 Push Steps deeper and angles inside, landing his second Jab.

Fighter 1 Exits the Exchange by Pivoting to stay sideways and steps back out of range.

Roundhouse to Jab

This one is a favorite of GSP, who dominated for years with the simple but brilliant use of jabs, level changes, and lead leg roundhouse kicks to the leg. Don't worry, I haven't forgotten the Superman Punch combinations, check out the Advanced section of this chapter. The two movements work well together, particularly if you can throw your Lead Leg Roundhouse Kicks off of a Pendulum Shuffle.

(Above) Fighter 1 leans forward to load weight for the Pendulum Shuffle.

Half way through the Pendulum Shuffle. Fighter 1 Feints Jab to get Fighter 2 to look up.

Fighter 1 connects with his foot rather than his shin, staying out of punching range.

Fighter 1 pushes deeper Inside off of his Rear Foot to change position.

Fighter 1 now Pivots off his Lead Foot. He is safely sideways, while Fighter 2 is still open facing away from Fighter 1.

Example: GSP – Any Fight (GSP throws this in reverse as well. Keep in mind he almost always throws the first move as a feint, not in full extension as shown here.)

Fighter 1 lands his jab and then Exits Offline.

GSP used the jab and lead leg roundhouse to the leg in conjunction with level change feints almost exclusively to set up his takedowns and power shots. If you have great feints and preparatory footwork, these two moves are nearly all you need from long range. However, such a simplistic style requires insane skill.

Body & Head Jab

Body Jabs are highly underrated. They suck power out of the opponent, paying off later in the fight. Combined with leg kick, they can drain the energy from the opponent like a syphon.

Example: Sugar Ray Leonard vs Floyd Mayweather (The body jab destroys your opponent's stamina and the head jab takes away his vision.)

(Above) Bother Fighters are On Line.

Having conditioned Fighter 2 to expect Jabs to the head, Fighter 1 instead catches him with his hands too high, digging into his solar plexus.

Fighter 2 is now thinking low, but Fighter 1 goes high.

Head & Body Jab

Just mixing a low-high combination with a high-low combination will create a whole lot of confusion for your opponent. Robinson, Leonard, and Ali all did this beautifly. All three would use cross steps and hop steps to achieve the same positions. There are certain advantages to this pattern, although it does come with it's own risks.

Pattern 5 - Online to Outside 3 To Outside 2

This Pattern usually results from a fighter turning into their lead hook a bit too much. Fighters like Joe Frazier, Mike Tyson and Rocky Marciano would leap into their lead hooks, often resulting on their lead leg moving outside their opponent's. This would usually be seen as a bad position, but all of aforementioned fighters listed became adept at pivoting hard off of their lead leg upon landing to throw with their rear hand. This actually resulted in a superior angle from the outside on many occasions. In fact, Rocky Marciano landed a great knockout off of this pattern.

Long Hook Pivot Outside Cross (Marciano KO)

Example: Rocky Marciano vs Ezzard 2 (This is not something to try to set up, but Marciano landed a KO this way when he found himself there by accident.)

(Above) Bother Fighters Online

Example 2: Joe Frazier (Frazier had a tendency to over-rotate on his lead hook, but was able to pivot out of it into a cross.)

Fighter 1 Steps his Lead Foot Outside as he throws a Long Hook.

Fighter 1 Pivots hard off his lead leg to connect from the Outside.

Just A Quick Reminder That Positioning Your Lead Foot Outside Your Opponents Is A Great Way To Set Up Spinning Attacks….

Spin Back Kick

Spin Back Fist

Or Trip and Sweep Like Machida

Pattern 6

This Pattern is a great introduction on how to change positional strategy mid combination. You start off aggressively moving deep Inside. As mentioned repeatedly (because it's really, really important) you can only stay in one position for so long before your opponent adjusts. It is in your best interest to never let your opponent regain their balance. Once they are able to plant down and throw with complete awareness of the situation, you are in extreme danger. This makes your Superior Position no longer Superior but simply more open.

After a few shots inside (three tops), it is time to adjust. As your opponent adjusts, you must proactively move first, L-Stepping Outside.

Mid Range Jab Cross to Close Range Angle Change

Example: McGregor vs Brimage KO Exchange (McGregor moved across the centerline, inside and outside, several times in the last exchange of the fight.)

(Above) Both Fighters Online

Fighter 1 Steps into Closed Inside 1 Position to Jab.

Fighter 1 Steps into Closed Inside 2 Position to land a Cross.

Fighter 2 adjusts by turning and sinking his weight, but Fighter 1 has wisely changed positions by L-Stepping to Closed Outside Position 1, as he prefers to be conscious.

Henry Armstrong Tactics

Henry Armstrong was one of the greatest boxers to ever live. His strategy was simple but effective. He would take a Close, Outside Position and drive his head into his opponent's chest or lead shoulder. He would continuously wrestler his opponents, knocking them off balance as he circled to the Outside. From this position, he could smother his opponent's attacks, land Body Hooks Inside, and Kidney and Head Hooks to the Outside.

Example: Henry Armstrong (Any Fight.)

(Above) Fighter 1 smothers Fighter 2 at Close Range.

Fighter 1 moves Outside, landing a Body Hook. He can continue moving Outside so long as Fighter 2 remains one step behind him.

Pattern 7

- Closed Inside 1 to Closed Inside 2 to Closed Inside 4 (Parallel) to D'Amato Shift

This is probably the most aggressive Footwork Pattern there is. It's used by some of the gutsiest fighters out there, like Mike Tyson or Demetrious Johnson. The idea is to move deep inside, squaring you up with your opponent. When following this strategy, you are either counting on staying one step ahead of your opponent, like Mighty Mouse. Or you are counting on simply being better than your opponent, like Tyson.

If you are going to use this Pattern, I would highly recommend using it as a transition to land a few strikes, like Dominick Cruz; or to escape the cage, like Johnson. If you do decide to go the Tyson route, remember that you are essentially putting yourself and your opponent in equally dangerous situations and betting on the fact that you will come out triumphant. This takes amazing footwork and every kind of defense. I am sure we are all familiar with the clip of Tyson dodging near 10 punches in place before landing a KO with a well placed Hook. Saying that is not something that can be done easily would be understating it greatly.

Square Up & Throw

(Above) Both Opponents Online

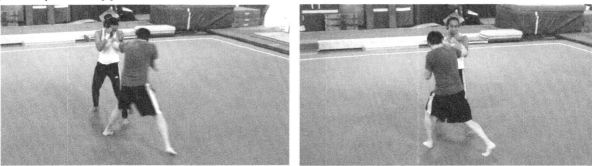

Fighter 1 throws a 1-2, ending in Closed Inside 2.

Example: Mike Tyson vs Lorenzo Canady 1st Knockdown

Fighter 1 Shuffles deeper Inside to a Parallel Position, squared up with Fighter 2. They are both wide open to nearly all attacks.

Fighter 1 must now rely on superior defense and countering skills to win the Exchange.

Fighter 1 Jump Turns to D' Amato Shift into a Rear Hook. Bother Fighters have transitioned to Southpaw, but Fighter 1 is counting on the fact that they are comfortable in this stance, while Fighter 2 is not.

Fighter 1 Exits with a parting shot, throwing a Lead Roundhouse kick before Pendulum Shuffling backwards out of the Exchange (a favorite of Mighty Mouse).

Pattern 8

Max Holloway consistently lands with this Footwork Pattern. The concept is the same as Pattern 6, but instead of Angling Outside to remain Close, you will Laterally Cross Step out of an Inside Exchange to land a Spinning attack off of your Rear Side. This is the last example for Closed Stance Footwork Patterns. If I've done my job well, you should be thinking about new possibilities for strikes to land off of these Patterns, or even new ways to combine these Patterns, concepts and strategies to try for yourself.

Jab Cross Inside to Shuffle Back To Step Outside Spin Back Kick

Example: Max Holloway vs Will Chope.

(Above) Both Fighters Online

Fighter 1 Enters Inside with a Jab Cross

Before Fighter 2 can adjust, Fighter 1 Shuffles back with a Lead Hook to Cover their adjustment.

194

Fighter 1 Cross Steps to Outside Position 3, setting up a Spinning Attack. This lets them catch their opponent if they tries to Exit Inside, or better yet, if they tries to Close Distance on Fighter 1 by moving forward.

Fighter 1 scores a spin back kick to Fighter 2's liver. A Spin Back Fist or Elbow would work just as well, depending on distance.

Open Sequences

Pattern 1

When it comes to footwork in the Open Position, it seems that the one thing everything knows is "Lead Foot Dominance". There is a reason for this: the position of the Lead Foot in Open Stances Exchanges is vitally important. Positioning the Lead Foot on the outside of your opponent's aligns your rear hand and foot with your opponent's Center Line, and lets you exit exchanges easily by moving to the Outside.

However, is has been a bit over emphasized. There are other Superior Positions in Open Stance Engagements, and keeping your Lead Foot on the Inside can have major benefits, if you know what you are doing.

But before we get to that, lets take a look at some ways to use the all-important "Lead Foot Dominance" Patterns.

Online To Open Outside 1 Position

Jab Cross Example

Fighter 1 Jabs While Online.

This Draws a Jab from Fighter 2, and Fighter 1 Ducks under, Stepping his Lead Foot to the Open Outside 1 Position.

With Guard Pull

Lead Hand control is vitally important when in an Open Stance, as both you and your opponent's lead arms are aligned on the same side. It can be hard to land around this obstacle, so Guard Manipulation can be a valuable tool. Lomachenko manages to consistently pull down or pin his opponent's lead arm. In MMA this is much easier due to the open finger gloves.

It is often best to land a jab or hook to cover distance, so Fighter 1 makes sure to land their Jab on the opponent's guard rather than the head or body.

Fighter 1 now pulls down Fighter 2's Lead Arm, exposing the face. This should usually be done at the same time an attack is thrown, but it is shown independently here for clarity.

Fighter 1 now Steps Outside to align their Rear Hand with Fighter 2's Centerline.

Lead Roundhouse Enter To Open Outside 1, Cross To Rear Leg Roundhouse To Stomach

Lead Leg Roundhouse Kicks can be thrown to the opponent's leg from long range while maintaining your balance. This will pester the opponent, and hopefully tempt them to check your kick (leaving them stationary so you can close in) or draw an attack which you can counter.

Fighter 1 connects with a Lead Leg Roundhouse Kick, then Steps Back.

Fighter 2 moves in, and Fighter 1 quickly Steps Outside to throw a Cross.

Example: Saenchai or Andy Hug (Southpaws will often "glue" their rear and lead leg kicks together off of their cross.)

Fighter 2 is able to Block Fighter 1's Cross, but now their Guard is raised. Fighter 1 capitalizes by throwing a Rear Leg Roundhouse Kick to the ribs.

Pattern 2

Online To Open Outside 1 Position to Open Outside 2 Position

This Pattern is useful for connecting with something at close to mid range and then Exiting with a powerful Long Range attack. This Pattern was commonly used by Roy Jones Jr. and is still used today by movement fighters who rely on their speed and quick reflexes. In fact, if you are fast enough, you can simply step into Open Outside 2 Position to land a shot before Angling Outside to Exit. This does take incredible speed to pull off.

Jab To Body Hook

Fighter 1 Steps Outside to throw a Jab or Lead Hook to raise Fighter 2's Guard.

Fighter 1 then Steps deep Outside at a near 45 degree angle to set up a body hook.

Fighter 1 can now Pivot Outside to Exit, or Shuffle past Fighter 2 to perform an Outside D' Amato Shuffle like Roy Jones Jr.

Jab, Step Out Roundhouse To Leg Kick

Example: Changpuek Ketsongrit vs Rick Roufus (A historically important fight.)

Fighter 1 looks to set up an attack from an Outside position, but Fighter 2 moves Inside to avoid it and land his own attack.

Roufus switched to a southpaw stance after Changpuek destroyed his left leg. He then destroyed Roufus's right leg with this pattern, ending in a KO.

In response, Fighter 1 Steps further Outside to stay defensive and lands a Rear Leg Roundhouse Kick from a safe distance. Fighter 1 can now Exit safely.

Pattern 3

Online To Open Outside 1 Position to Open Outside 3 Position

This is the same concept as Closed Pattern 6, the Henry Armstrong example. The idea is to circle outside, forcing your opponents to turn while you pummel them or take them down. Because being in an Open Position makes it much easier to circle Outside, it results in some incredibly powerful techniques becoming readily available. It goes without saying that Lomachenko uses these tactics religiously. As does Max Holloway, who often Shifts into an Open Position to maneuver around his opponent's weak side.

Expose Opponents Weak Side At Close Range

Example: Max Holloway vs Cub Swanson

(Above) Fighter 1 and Fighter 2 are Online.

Fighter 1 Steps Outside to Jab.

Fighter 1 keeps their hand in place, bending their arm to pin Fighter 2's Lead Arm.

Fighter 1 lands a Body Hook with the Rear Hand. Fighter 2 Pivots Inside to reposition themselves to attack. But Fighter 1 leans in to smother Fighter 2 with their Rear Shoulder and protects the head by placing it on Fighter 2's Lead Shoulder.

Fighter 1 Pivots and Shuffles Outside again, once again exposing Fighter 2's weak side. The more drastic the skill difference between the two fighters, the longer Fighter 1 can remain on the Outside without Disengaging.

Pattern 4

Online to Open Inside Position 1 to Open Outside Position 1

Now is a great time to mention that positioning the Lead Foot Inside the opponents can bring major advantages, if you know how to use it. Perhaps the greatest proponent of this Position was Pernell Whitaker. The secret to Open Inside Position 1 is that is lines your Lead Hand up with your opponent's Centerline. That means it has a shorter distance to travel and hits harder than your opponent's lead hand that, in this Position, is on the Outside. Although your opponent's Rear Hand is in a better position to land than yours, you can mitigate this through adjusting your Angle, or simply landing with your Jab before they have a chance to land their Cross.

<u>Jab Inside to Cross Outside</u>

Example: **Pernell Whitaker vs Julio Cesar Chavez (Whitaker had complete mastery of these angles.)**

(Above) Both Fighters are Online, no advantage to either.

Both Fighters Jab, but Fighter 1's Lead Foot is Inside, allowing them to land first.

Having established an Inside Jab, Fighter 1 now Steps Back, and then Push Steps Forward.

This time, Fighter 1 positions his Lead Foot Outside, aligning their Rear Hand to land.

Taking advantage of Inside and Outside attacks rather than obsessing on the Outside Positions lends more depth to your game, and confuses your opponent to no end. There is nothing more discouraging than having an opponent who lands in positions where you believe yourself to be safe or dominant.

Pattern 5

Online to Open Inside Position 1 to Pivot Out

I had mentioned Pernell Whitaker before, and rightly so. He was an absolute master of footwork in an Open Stance, being a Southpaw in a sport full to the brink with Orthodox fighters. One of his most useful techniques was his ability to Circle Outside while placing his Lead Foot Inside to land with his Lead Hand. While this may seem counterproductive, or even dangerous, the examples below will clarify why this seeming contrast in principles worked so well.

Circle & Jab Inside To Pivot Outside

Fighter 1 has been Circling Outside, while Fighter 2 has been attempting to take an Outside Position. Fighter 1 lets them have it, Stepping Inside with their Lead Foot to land a Jab. Fighter 2's Jab misses, finishing Outside of Fighter 1's Jab.

Example: Once again, Pernell Whitaker (If you are a southpaw, I would suggest watching every fight.)

Fighter 2 is now in the perfect position to land a Cross, but Fighter 1 changes Angles, Pivoting Outside. Fighter 2 can no longer reach them, and is too fully committed to their attack to quickly change positions.

Fighter 1 can now Exit safely by Stepping or Shuffling Back.

Pattern 5A

This same pattern can be used with Open Outside Position 1, Pivoting Outside with your Lead Foot already in position to do so. However, you will want to negate your opponent's lead hand before doing so, as shown in Pattern 1.

Fighter 1 Pivots Outside after landing a Cross by Stepping Outside. They should be wary of Fighter 2's Lead Hand when doing so. This time, they were able to time Fighter 2's Cross, meaning the Lead Hand Jab was not a serious threat.

Pattern 6

Online to Open Inside Position 1 to Open Inside Position 2

This is a difficult Position to attain, but can be highly effective for Rear Side attacks. Fighters who have used it to with great success include Zab Judah and Conor McGregor. The idea is to gain a position Far Inside to land with a power shot. You should be sideways, and your opponent should be wide open, destroying their ability to balance and making it near impossible to guard every last part of themselves. Despite the advantages the transition Inside can be very dangerous.

Jab Cross

Example: Roy Jones Jr vs Richard Frazier and Richard Hall (This is how Jones dealt with southpaws. It works equally well in an open stance with either foot forward, ie. Rigondeaux.)

(Above) Both Fighters are On Line, with their feet Even.

Fighter 1 Steps Inside to Jab. In response, Fighter 2 moves to Pivot Outside.

Fighter 1 now quickly Steps in deeper and Pivots Inside.

Zab was having a lot of success with this technique against Mayweather, until Mayweather began Shifting Inside to smother Zab, blocking him from getting the Inside Angle first.

Intermediate Footwork Patterns

Concept 1- Enter Off Of Linear Leg Kicks

Closed On Line Position Kick-Shift To Open Outside 1

Kick-Shifts to the leg add a whole new element of unpredictability for your opponent. After you connect, you can drive your foot down to land Inside or Outside in nearly any angle.

Example: All of these sequences can be observed in Max Holloway's fights. (Most other fighters are far behind in regards to leg kicks, using linear kicks as distance keepers instead of a means to enter.)

Closed Online Position Feint Kick-Shift to Draw Feint to Wrist Control to Open Outside 3 Hook D'Amato Shift

Once your kick is established as a threat, you can feint it to cause your opponent to check. Every time your opponent lifts their leg to check, they are left temporarily immobile for a split second. This is when you have the chance to step in deep.

Fighter 1 Feints a Leg Teep To Draw a Check from Fighter 2.

Now that Fighter 2 has Checked, they are stuck in place, and Fighter 1 can move deep Outside.

212

Fighter 1 Grabs Fighter 2's Wrist.

Fighter 1 pulls down Fighter 2's Guard and lands deep inside, landing a Lead Hook.

Fighter 1 D'Amato Shifts Outside to Exit

Closed Online Kick-Shift To Open Outside 1 Position Pivot Out Lead Hook

Open Online Kick-Shift to Closed Inside 2 to Land Cross Pivot to Closed Inside 3 and Hook to Exit

Fighter 1 lands a Teep on Fighter 2's Lead Leg, loading up his Rear Hand.

Fighter 1 lands their Lead Leg deep Inside, connecting with their Cross.

Fighter 1 Pivots into Closed Inside 3 Position to land a Long Hook and Exit.

Concept 2 - Moving From Inside to Outside & Outside to Inside

Throw a 1-2 in Closed Inside 2 then Switch-Shift to Open Outside 1 Throw Rear Leg Roundhouse Kick To Solar Plexus

Using Switch Shifts mid combination can create openings for power shots that would not be available otherwise. If there is an opening for your Lead Hand or Foot, quickly turning it into your Rear Hand or Foot by switching you stance and add a lot of power to your blow.

Fighter 1 Steps in deep to land a 1-2.

Example: TJ Dillashaw vs Mike Easten Round 2 4:22 Left (Or Dillashaw vs Barao 1 Round 4 4:35 left for a head kick example. Dillashaw uses this same pattern in every fight, but has several different strikes he throws off of it.)

Fighter 1 Switch-Shifts Outside to land a Cross off of their new Rear Hand.

Fighter 1 finishes with a Rear Leg Roundhouse Kick to Fighter 2's stomach.

Enter with a Switch Shift Rebound into Open Outside 1 then Pivot-Shuffle to Open Outside 3

Switch Shift Rebounds are one of the quickest ways to transition to a superior position on the other side of the opponent's centerline. By mastering this technique, you can make equal use of both Inside and Outside superior positions.

Fighter 1 Switches their feet and Rebounds off of their new Rear Foot to angle a Cross.

Example: Dom Cruz vs Scott Jorgenson Round 1 2:00 left. (Cruz uses this same pattern off of a V-Shift.)

Fighter 1 immediately shuffles deeper Outside.

Closed On Line Side Lunge to Inside Neutral then Pivot Inside to Open Inside 3 to Land Hook.

Fighter 1 Side Lunges off of their lead leg to cut across Inside.

Fighter 1 Pivots to a safer position and Shuffles back to Exit.

Closed On Line to Land 1-2 in Open Inside 2 then Side Lunge Body Hook to Closed Outside 2 Pivot Out To Exit with Lead Hook

This combination is a great example of how one extremely risky position can result in transferring to a safer, more superior position. Side Lunges are a risky buy highly rewarding technique to master.

Fighter 1 Steps Inside to land a 1-2.

Fighter 2 throws a Long Hook, but Fighter 1 cuts across and ducks under, landing a Body Hook.

Example: Willie Pep vs Ray Famechon Round 9.

Fighter 1 Exits by Pivoting with their Lead Hook.

Lead Hand Superman Punch Lateral Shuffle to Land Lead Roundhouse Kick

This is GSP's signature combination. As the opponent tried to move away from GSP's Superman Punch, GSP would shuffle Outside to catch them with a hard leg kick, loaded with the momentum from his Superman Punch.

Example: GSP vs Josh Koscheck 2nd Round 1:15 left.

Rear Hand Superman Punch Lateral Shuffle to Land Lead Roundhouse Kick

Example: GSP vs Josh Koscheck 3ʳᵈ Round 0:37 left. (GSP used this pattern in most of his fights.

V - Shifting to Cut Off the Opponent

Example: Watch Pep, Cruz or Mighty Mouse for V-Shifts. This pattern is a good drill to practice using the V-Shift to create angles and intercept the opponent.

Enter into an exchange any way you like, and then have your partner try to turn and pivot away while you V-Shift to take superior angles.

Fighter 1 Pendulum Shuffles to land a Lead Leg Roundhouse Kick on Fighter 2's Lead Leg.

Fighter 1 lands their leg inside to angle in a Cross.

Fighter 1 Pivots Out and Steps Back, but Fighter 2 is balanced and moves in to attack.

In response, Fighter 1 slides their lead leg back, beginning to V-Shift.

Fighter 1 completes the V-Shift and land a Rear Body Hook.

Fighter 2 tries to Exit by Stepping Inside to throw a Cross.

But Fighter 1 V-Shifts again, Slipping Fighter 2's Cross and connecting with a Lead Hook.

Advanced Footwork Patterns

Multiple Lateral & Parallel Angle Changes & Shifts

Side Lunge to Outside Neutral Turn Shuffle

(Above) Fighter 1 and Fighter 2 are Online.

Fighter 1 Side Lunges Outside, connecting with a long, looping Hook.

Fighter 1 Turn Shuffle smoothly to connect with a Cross.

Switch Shift Rebound Shuffle Outside Rebound to Outside Neutral

Example: Sugar Sean O'Malley vs Andre Soukhamthath Round 2 3:32 left. (Switch Shift Enter added for fun.)

Fighter 1 Switch Shifts to land a Cross from Southpaw.

Fighter 1 drags their Rear Leg forward to Neutral, then Turn Shuffles to Outside Neutral.

Fighter 1 Rebounds off their Rear Foot to land a Cross from Outside.

Open Stance Side Lunge to Neutral Turn Shuffle to Inside Neutral D'Amato Shift Exit *(Dominick Cruz)*

Fighter 1 Side Lunges to land a wide Rear Hook.

Fighter 1 Turn Shuffles to land a tight Cross.

Fighter 1 D'Amato Shift Exits Inside.

Side Lunge Outside Rebound to Closed Outside 1 Shift to Open Outside 2

Example: Wonderboy Thompson vs Masvidal Knockdown (Second Round 3:40 Left)

Fighter 1 cuts Outside, then Rebounds off their right leg.

Fighter 1 lands a Cross from Closed Outside 1, then Shifts forward.

Fighter 1 land a Rear Cross as they Shift Forward.

Side Lunge Inside Rebound Shift Into Open Inside 1 (TJ Dillashaw)

Example: TJ Dillashaw vs Issei Tamura KO

Fighter 1 Half Shifts back and Rebounds Inside.

Fighter 1 connects with a Rear Leg Roundhouse.

Step to Closed Inside 2 Half Shift to Inside Neutral Bounce Pivot to Open Inside 3

Example: Wonderboy Thompson vs Masvidal

240

Fighter 1 Steps deep Inside at a wide angle.

Fighter 1 Half Shift Into Inside Neutral and Bounces into a sideways, Southpaw Stance.

Fighter 2 moves forward to chase, but Fighter 1 Back Kicks to the solar plexus and runs out to Exit.

Side Lunge to Inside Neutral Half Shift to Open Inside 1 Step Through D'Amato Shift to Exit

Fighter 1 Side Lunges to Inside Neutral at Mid Range.

Fighter 2 Shells Up and starts to reposition, but Fighter 1 Half Shifts forward and lands an Uppercut through Fighter 2's Guard.

Fighter 1 D'Amato Shifts to land a Rear Hook and then Steps Through to Exit.

Switch-Shift to Neutral, Rebound Inside, Turn Shuffle to D'Amato Shift

Thanks for reading.

Please feel free to email me with any questions at:

 TheMMArts@gmail.com.

Or follow me on Twitter:

@MMArtist

You can see full video breakdowns of techniques, fights and fighters at:

https://www.youtube.com/c/TheModernMartialartist.

If you enjoyed this book, please leave a positive review!

Happy Training,

David

Made in the USA
Monee, IL
31 August 2023

41903346R00138